Lost and Found in Acadie

Clive Doucet

NIMBUS
PUBLISHING

Nimbus Publishing Limited
PO Box 9166
Halifax, NS   B3K 5M8
(902) 455-4286

Printed and bound in Canada
Interior design: Denise Williams
Cover design: Margaret Issenman
Author photo: Yanishevsky Tardioli Photography, Ottawa

Library and Archives Canada Cataloguing in Publication

Doucet, Clive, 1946-
Lost and found in Acadie / Clive Doucet.
ISBN 1-55109-482-7

1. Acadians. 2. Acadians—Ethnic identity. 3. Acadians—History.
4. Acadia. I. Title.

FC2041.D677 2004   971.5'004114   C2004-903837-0

Canada   The Canada Council | Le Conseil des Arts
for the Arts | du Canada

We acknowledge the financial support of the Government of Canada through the Book Publishing Industry Development Program (BPIDP) and the Canada Council for our publishing activities.

CONTENTS

*To be lost and found in Acadie is also to be lost
    and found on our planet,*
*with all of its prosperities and poverties, comings
    and goings,*
peoples and languages, religions and nations.
*To be found is to be confident that we all have a
    bright future.*
To be lost is to despair for any future at all.

Beginning

"Elle est retrouvée
—Quoi?—L'éternité
c'est la mer
allée avec le soleil"

It is found again.
—What?—Eternity
It is the sea
gone with the sun.

—Arthur Rimbaud

Ialways knew that I would one day write a book about my grandfather. I knew it from the time we drove down to the Co-op by the harbour in the buggy. The old mare clip-clopped briskly over the asphalt, her great splayed hooves smashing out their own tune, the buggy's steel-rimmed wheels rattling so loudly that we sounded like a parade. On one side of the road, the ocean stretched towards Rimbaud's infinity, and on the other, soft, green fields climbed toward the mountains. The wonder of that grand scene would have stirred even the dullest soul, but it was more than the landscape that made me think about one day trying to get down on paper what I was seeing and feeling. Even as a young boy, I understood that the kind of life my grandfather lived was disappearing.

In the 1930s, when my father had been growing up in the village, every house had a small barn and stable behind it, and even the priest drove about the parish in his horse and buggy. But by the 1950s, the car and the tractor were quickly displacing farmers like grandfather, who tilled the soil on small farms with horse-drawn tools. Grandfather still made money every year selling cream to the dairy, cattle to the local butcher, and potatoes, turnips, and oats to the Co-op. But looming on the horizon were vast, mechanized dairy barns stocked with giant Holsteins that never moved from their stalls. Their udders would be attached twice a day to piped mechanical systems that pumped milk into billion-dollar multi-national companies. These industrial farms would wipe out the local dairies, and agro-businesses like McCain's and Pharmalat would extinguish the local markets. Small dairies, cheese factories, butchers and markets would dissolve into memory.

By today's standards, farms like my grandfather's were not much more than large gardens. Grandfather's farm was only about eighty acres, its most prominent feature a shingled barn painted red and edged with a white trim. By today's standards, it looked like a toy barn. The farm itelf ran in a long, narrow line from the sea coast right up to the mountains, with upland pastures in the highlands for the young cattle, and hayfields and potato and turnip crops in the fields closer to the sea. He had a small, mixed herd of dairy and beef cattle, pigs and chickens loitering by the barn and, down by the pond, a small apple orchard.

Grandfather and Grandmother had raised ten children on their little farm, and even in the darkest moments of the great Depression, everyone had been fed, clothed and housed. But my father's generation had abandoned the farm for the city and it was clear even to a young boy that once these tough, old men gave up their farms, there would be no one to replace them. The farms and all the intricate, seasonal mechanisms that kept them so fruitful would wind down and blow away—back into conifers and scrub.

I loved farming. For me there was no better way to spend the day than to follow Grandfather around as he went from morning milking at first light to splitting "small wood" for the kitchen stove at the end of the day. It was there that I learned that the universe was composed not of molecules but stories, stories about how to build a road through the bush or a mill by a stream, stories about a defrocked priest, stories about my uncles and aunts, stories of heroes and villans.

Farm work is often portrayed as monotonous, but I never found it so. The clever independence of the farm and all its arrangements fascinated me from the moment I first walked out toward the barn to milk the cows. In the warm, hay-perfumed stalls, the cows seemed like magical creatures in their ability to produce buckets and buckets of pure, foaming milk. The barn cats would watch us milk, waiting patiently for what they knew would be their small portion. The barn was the opposite of the house, tranquil and purposeful, and I slid into its life.

Grandfather never bought commercial fertilizer at the Co-op. *"Ça fatigue la terre, et en plus ça coute trop"* (it exhausts the land plus it's costly). Instead, he had a boggy area, not far from the barn, in which he had built a soft dome of gestating loam layered with fish guts, seaweed, earth and manure, which would cook all year long, creating a rich, organic fertilizer. One of our frequent chores was to keep building it up at one end and taking the "cooked" fertilizer from the other. Everywhere we spread the fertilizer—in the garden, in the potato and turnip fields—the crops

The harvests were rich, and each fall hay and oats and potatoes and turnips filled the barn.

grew quickly and well. The harvests were rich, and each fall hay and oats and potatoes and turnips filled the barn.

In the barn, there was a heavy, cast-iron machine, the likes of which I've never seen except in a museum. We operated it with a crank. Inside the machine were sharp blades that sliced the turnips into shreds, which Grandfather mixed with oats and barley to create a homemade silage that the cows could digest easily. Consequently, the pails brimmed with sweet tasting milk all year long.

Grandfather sold all his produce "against the season." He never sold at harvest time, when the prices were low. A small farm will never make anyone rich, but it can provide a living. On Grandfather's farm, nothing was wasted, not even work. "Why work hard, when you don't have to?" Grandfather would ask. It was not that he was averse to hard work—he was wiry and strong, and at seventy-eight, could pitch hay all day. It was that when profits were so small, the return on effort had to be maximized.

Our carts, trucks, and equipment were all kept in sheds so they would not be damaged by the weather and would require as few repairs as possible. Grandfather had a workshop where he could repair harnesses and grind cutting bars. He could do everything but shoe the horses and build wheels. Horses had to go to the blacksmith and wheels to the cartwright. All this seemed more interesting to me than the Crown Jewels, glinting behind their bars in the Tower of London.

A small farm had everything that I cherished: independence, a variety of endeavours, and vivid connections with nature, but when I expressed an interest in becoming a farmer, Grandfather laughed and dismissed it in a sentence: "The time of the small farms is gone." And so I put away my ambitions of being a farmer. How could he be wrong? He had sent all eight of his sons out into the world to earn a living elsewhere, asking not one of them to stay.

I did eventually write about those summers in Cape Breton, but not until I was married with children of my own and far from any possibility of ever being a farmer. *My Grandfather's Cape Breton* was written after Grandfather had died, in six weeks of intense effort. It became the most successful book that I would write, but what I didn't understand then was that this brief account of a young boy's summers with his grandfather would be just the first step in a much longer, harder journey: unravelling the history of Acadie.

The deportation of the Acadian people began in 1755 and continued until 1764, when the Seven Years' War between the French and the British concluded. But at the end of the war, the Acadians were not included in the peace treaty. It was as if they had never existed. They were not allowed to return and reclaim their lands.

It was illegal for them to come home. Those who did return were forced to do so clandestinely, settling in remote parts of Maritime Canada, in Cape Breton and the Madawaska region of New Brunswick, away from contact with new European settlers. Once they were evicted, their houses, barns, farms and churches around the Bay of Fundy were burnt to the ground and their lands were given to those who were prepared to bear arms for the British Crown.

It slowly became clear to me that a nation's history is rarely about what actually happened. It's mostly about the struggle of one side to dominate another. The national memory of this struggle belongs to the winners and the Acadians belonged to one of the losing sides, so they dropped out of the books. Unlike the Mi'kmaq and the Métis of western Canada, they did not fight for their right to hold their lands and retain their culture. The reason for the expropriation of their lands and deportation was their continued refusal to choose a side and bear arms for either the British or the French. Although the Acadians recognized British sovereignty, and provisioned and billeted British forces, they refused to bear arms against either their neighbours the Mi'kmaq or the Canadiens on behalf of the British crown. This was never considered acceptable by the British colonial authorities; in the eighteenth century, farmers didn't take independent political stances.

I grew up with little real understanding of exactly why my grandfather's village was located in the remotest part of a remote island. Acadian history was not taught in school. Indeed, it would have seemed exotic and a little bizarre to my Ontario high school teachers that any of their students could name grandfathers and grandmothers six generations back who had been deported from Canada. Acadian history was treated as the stuff of myth, much as aboriginal history has been relegated to the mists of legend. But this is not legend or myth. It is woven into the fabric of peoples' lives in long, complicated threads, barely noticed

I never planned on becoming "an Acadian writer." If I had any literary ambition, it was to become the house poet for *The New Yorker*. But after writing *My Grandfather's Cape Breton*, it was as if I were being dragged against my will, back, like a compass needle, to the only point where I could rest. Sometimes it was in poetry.

Sometimes it was in prose. Often it took me down unexpected paths.

I will never forget walking around the Métis village of Batoche with the Saskatchewan poet Glenn Sorestad. The village is high above the Saskatchewan River, and an old, white, clapboard church still stands with bullet holes augured into the steeple from the last battle against the Métis. It is a simple building that looks very much like the old church in my grandfather's village. Before that moment, it had never occurred to me that the Métis people had lived as we did in Grand Étang—with a church, a little school and their farms arranged in rows or "rangs" beside each other so that each farmer had equal access to the river front or the sea. I thought the Métis were buffalo hunters and lived much the same as Indians.

As I walked around the old fields and farm lanes of Batoche, it didn't feel foreign to me. It felt like home and this realization carried a tremendous emotional impact. Suddenly I was aware of profound connections between what happened to the Métis and what happened to the Acadians. Both had been an independent, North American people; both were an original and unique blend of the Old World and the New; both thought they had inalienable rights to their communities, language and way of life by virtue of the lands they had occupied, their connections to the aboriginal nations, and their strong view of themselves as a people. And both suffered immensely for their refusal to simply bow their heads and comply with the wishes of the dominant culture.

I came home from Batoche exhilarated by these discoveries and spent the next five years writing a long, narrative poem called "Looking for Henry." Henry Letendre was a Métis artist that I had gone looking for in the Saskatoon marketplace where he sold his paintings from the back of a truck. I had seen some of his paintings in the publishing house I was visiting and had been impressed, but I never found him. He was always elsewhere. As I wrote the poem, however, I found out about him. I learned he was a descendant of Leandre Letendre, the founder of the village of Batoche. And gradually "Looking for Henry" became my song to the Métis People, to the Acadians, and to the story of displacement we shared. The poem itself became my own vehicle of discovery, for in composing it, I discovered that there were Mi'kmaw grandmothers in the Doucet family tree, something I had never known.

When I asked my father why he had never mentioned that the Doucettes at Eskasoni, an Indian reservation not far from our village, were related to us, he just shrugged and said he supposed it wasn't *à la mode* when he was young to admit you had aboriginal connections. This severing of relations between the Acadians and the Mi'kmaq was one of the many ways in which the deportation deformed and changed Acadian history. Afterwards, even though it was the Mi'kmaq who saved Acadian escapees of the deportation, the relations were never the same. Both groups of people were focused on surviving, and the old connections extinguished.

I am not Mi'kmaq, but it is important to know that I have Mi'kmaw grandmothers because I would not be here, and would not be who I am, without them. To be a whole human being we must recognize and honour all of our past, but to honour that past we must first know it existed. Without understanding our individual and collective history, we are all diminished. Trying to unravel my family's past has led me to many different places: Louisiana, Boston, Western Canada, California, and Maritime Canada. I have found many other people on the same voyage in all of these places.

CHAPTER ONE

Saying Goodbye

The village of Grand Étang
is perched on the ocean's edge
where the colours of the sunset
bleed in a great blaze upon the sea;
until the flames of the spreading, disappearing
  sun
are written forever in the eye,
until the day folds up her wings and dusk arrives.
A place where the earth revolves in the night sky
towards the morning sun like a great toy ball,
and the day wakes in the hand as small as a
  thought.

The plane arced above Cape Breton. Below, there were no valleys, no villages, no fields or roads visible. The many small complexities that make a place human and not just geography vanish at 30,000 feet. There was just the form of the island traced in the sea from the highlands shrouded in clouds, down the long, sandy gulf shore to the Bras d'Or lakes, which cut through the centre leaving a white curl that marks the division between sea and land. I strained through the porthole to make out Kelly's Mountain, which sits in the middle of the island like a great signpost, but there was nothing. From 30,000 feet, Kelly's Mountain is just a change in colouring, the tip of the mountain showing gray against the surface of the island.

Cape Breton is not a small place. It is not like Prince Edward Island, which sits in the gulf, featureless and flat as a shoe's sole. Cape Breton is a piece of the continent broken off in the sea, with mountains and valleys, coal mines and lakes, and great cliffs where eagles glide along immense rock faces. It is an island on the tear line between the Old World and the New, and that tectonic tearing is visible everywhere: in the fishing grounds, estuaries and highland glens that feel like Scotland; in the coal mines that look like the coal mines of Wales; in the people who talk with accents that are neither entirely Scottish nor French but somewhere in between. Cape Breton has always been wild and hard. It is not a place that anyone calls home easily.

It is, no doubt, a strange thing to think of a place you've never really lived in for more than a few months at a time as home. But that is the way it has been for me. By the time I was born my father had already said his final goodbye to Cape Breton. Like thousands of young men and women before him, he had taken the road past Margaree Harbour, past Broad Chapel Cove, past Inverness and down the gulf shore, where the sea beckons around every headland to the ferry at Canso, and on to the mainland. Cape Breton became the place that my father was from, but not the place of his present or future.

My grandparents could not leave the farm, so all ten of their children journeyed back each summer to see them, towing their own children with them, like salmon making their way back from the sea to the river of their birth. My earliest memories are all mixed up with Cape Breton. It is like looking through a tiny crack in a door. I can see memère taking me to see the chickens. She is a tall woman, tall as a pine tree to my two-year-old eyes. Through that crack in memory's door, I can hear her voice. It is a soft Acadian voice and she is telling me a story.

It never occurred to me that my parents made a great effort to get our family back to the village. To small children, distances do not exist. Everything is written in the present tense. Where your parents are, where your grandparents are, those places *are* home and thus the memories of village life become written in the oldest, deepest places. The details have fled, but the sound of the old Acadian language can suddenly evoke a memory anchored so far in the past that tears spring to my eyes without my knowing why they are there.

The plane's jets roared with steady reassurance under the wings and suddenly Cape Breton was receding, winking out. For the first time, instead of Cape Breton leaving me, it was I who was setting the island aside, village by village, from cove to headland, from coastlines to mountains, back into the past, back into memory.

Maybe it was the effect of the funeral, but I felt older, as if in two short days I had finished some journey that I had started long ago, unaware.

My father sat by my side on the plane and I was grateful for his company. The winds that buffeted us both came not from the atmosphere, but from the relentless motion of time. As is his habit, my father disguised his feelings in a great deal of talk, but finally he was also silent, leaving me with the melancholy sense that it wasn't just my Uncle Joe who had passed on but that an entire generation was leaving us. Arthur is gone. Philias is gone. Joe is gone. Gerard is gone. I know Dad has started to count who is left and think about how long he might go on.

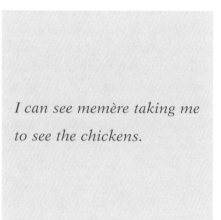

I can see memère taking me to see the chickens.

Listening to my father chatter away at the last funeral, it was

clear that he had jumped back into the past, back to the time when he and his brothers had all been together in a one-room school-house in Grand Étang, before they had left the village for the wider world. They were leaving again, but this time for a place infinitely farther away. I listened as I always did like a son, a little on the outside, a little on the inside.

When he's with family, Dad's old French rolls out as if he spoke it every day, the broad accents and antique words fitting perfectly with the stories I have now heard so many times that I think of them as part of my own past. Stories about a man who could run so fast he caught foxes by the tail, stories about Chandeleur parties and the Mi-Carême. Stories that have been polished and chiseled many times in the re-telling. I've heard the story too about how a snowstorm shut the roads down between the two villages and Father DeCoste took the Grand Étang choir in a convoy of sleighs all the way to Margaree Forks, how they went singing and hallowing and laughing over the fields that separated the two villages as the bright, white snow cascaded in curves from the sleighs' runners. At the funeral, Dad meets a priest at whose Ordination Mass he sang. Father Doyle is still tall and slim but he is now eighty-eight. Dad is seventy-eight; at the time of the young priest's ordination, he was just fifteen. They speak in a kind of wonderment at meeting so many years later, as if each is not sure what to do with such a strange event.

The plane engines droned on. I drifted off, content that I had been able to be with my father when he said goodbye to his older brother, and content to have seen my cousins again. I drifted on until I was back, sitting beside my grandfather as the cart bumped down the narrow road toward the bottom of the steep valley. The day was perfumed with summer, the smell of the horse, timothy grass at the edge of the road and small, crimson strawberries glinting in the green along the bank.

My father's generation is the last to speak French in a way that has remained unchanged since the time of Molière. In Acadian French, words and verbs are pronounced and conjugated differently than in modern French. My uncles say *j'avions*, not *j'ai*, *J'm'en vas*, not *Je m'en vais*. *On coumnence*, not *commence* en

Acadie. One is a *parsounne*, not a *personne* and so on. If you read an uncorrected version of a Molière play or the letters of Madame de Sevigny you will find it corresponds more closely to Acadian French than today's version of the language. But for my generation, it is the language of our elders, not our own.

My aunt Germaine and I sat together at the funeral. Aunt Germaine got along well with the dead. Once someone died, their status improved immeasurably. The longer they were dead, the better they were. Grandmother had graduated into sainthood in my aunt's eyes. In life, Uncle Philias had always been something of a reprobate, *un vieux garçon*—slow to marry, slow to take on adult responsibilities. In death, he became a good man. After enough time, he will graduate to a more favourable position and be remembered for driving my aunt to church and many other small favours.

Germaine never got along with her brothers and sisters, feeling bitter that they had managed to get more out of life than she had. She hadn't wanted a husband, school had bored her, and she didn't take to drink. With her volcanic anger, Aunt Germaine was at her most confident and powerful when she was threatening to throw herself off the cliffs into the sea: "*J'en ai assez! Le monde est pourri!*" (I've had enough! The world is rotten!) was one of her favourite sayings. Her petite stature was in utter contrast to words delivered with gale force, usually while she was still in her pyjamas, rocking at a vicious rate in her little chair by the radio. Although I can never remember Aunt Germaine making even the slightest move toward the door, Grandpa assured me that there had been occasions when he had to bar the door to stop her from running to the cliffs.

I lived with Aunt Germaine for three summers and learned to walk around her carefully. Grandfather and I would leave the house early in the morning to do the milking before she rose. We would clean up the milk separator together. Sometimes Aunt Germaine would help us, sometimes she wouldn't. Often, there was a heavy silence upon us as we worked because we were never sure what might trigger an eruption from her. I surely didn't want to be responsible for setting her off.

We spent our days out-of-doors in a kind of unspoken conspiracy that sought shelter from Aunt Germaine's sharp tongue and uncertain temper. Aunt Germaine could speak faster than any human being I have ever met. Her French was like lightning, and neither Grandfather nor I wanted to be struck. We could have been Indians, growing browner and browner as the summer progressed, always on the move, able to feel as easy on the land as if it were one vast living room. We returned to the house only to eat and sleep.

And yet somewhere under it all, somewhere there was a sweet soul, which now and then came scrabbling to life, as if she had been drowning and had surfaced, gasping for air. In these moments, she taught me things I'd never forget, like that mass was not about priests and dogma and ritual response, but about talking to God. "An hour a week to talk to God, that's not too much to ask, is it?" She understood instinctively without artifice what most did not.

My aunt is old now. Her legs refuse to work. After all these furious years, it is as if a switch has been thrown and all the anger, of nothing ever being right, of no one ever loving her enough, of nothing ever being good enough, has finally suffused, and she is left rocking quietly, overlooking the harbour still.

It is only at funerals that I see Dad with enough people around him to enter the places of his childhood. For a few days, his childhood becomes vivid again. The vibrant landscapes and complex web of uncles, aunts, brothers, sisters and cousins that once knitted the villages of the Acadian shore together rise in the form of these aged families and neighbours. It has to be reconstructed from memory for it is not just the people, but the landscape of the village that has also changed. There is scarcely a barn left. They have all been torn down and the timbers sold. The animals vanished.

In the heart of the village, where once the finest farms stood, a golf course has sprung up. Lawyers' offices deal with divorces, and the bars beam in Tiger Woods swinging through another tournament. The fishermen drive high-powered, diesel-engine boats and they cast their nets with hydraulic machinery. My cousins take tourists out to watch the whales. The sea like the land now has its tractors. Sixteen-wheel trucks now bring the village Co-op exotic fruits from distant places. There is still fiddle music; that is the one thing that has not changed.

At the funeral Aunt Germaine told me I was *têtu*—stubborn— and recounted how Grandfather had told me that the axe was sharp and to wait for him, but I had insisted on splitting the heavy wood alone, and for my pains buried the axe in my foot. An unlucky leg…it has more scars than I want. They run down each side of the shin, with a dent like a bullet hole in the middle where the bone came through from a skiing injury. The skin healed, but it's jumpy and shiny. The old wound where the axe cut through the boot is still there, but it's scarcely visible, nothing more than a faint, white line. Tétu, yes, I was. Tétu, I am.

My aunt smiles at me. She was always small, but now she is tiny, frail, and wheelchair bound. And I? I am unconscionably older. So old that my children are older than I was in my last summer on the farm. Aunt Germaine watches everything with the same quick, bird-like attention I remember. She misses nothing, eats little. She no longer seems angry at me for being tétu. It is as if the two of us have surfaced on the other side of the planet, and we are no longer quite the same people. She is calm. She seems happy. Time has bent us into new shapes and yet we are still what we are; my aunt is still my aunt, and I am still her nephew, and we both take comfort in that. I wonder if she wishes she were forty-seven and crazy again? Sometimes, I wish I were twelve again, just to smell the old wood stove, and feel a brand new day break against the shore.

There were always eagles over Carding Mill Road. They sailed down from the mountains, shadows against the sky, giving little, taking little, watching the progress of life, disinterested kings of another realm. Carding Mill Road clings to the edge of the mountain like a gravel stream, running down the cliff to the pond. It curves past the ruins of the old mill, past small houses and orchards, past woodlots, past the sawmill of my uncle, Gerard à William, then turns up into the mountains, to the winter chantiers, up into the distant places.

Grandfather and I are loading up the wagon with fence posts from my uncle's mill. Once the cart is full, we go to pick raspberries in the clearing at the back of our property. There is a warm, desultory richness to the day that remains even in my dreams, for Grandfather had arrived at the point in his life where he had no more obligations to run to, no more of life's alarms to raise. He took each day as it came, moment by moment like sips of tea. The horse's tail swishes back and forth against the flies. The rasp-

Sometimes on Carding Mill Road, it would seem that the world was perfect and everything was as it should be.

berry canes ripen in the summer heat. An eagle's shadow crosses our path. We crane our heads to look at the bird's silent glide.

There were cracks in the universe—I knew that even then. But sometimes on Carding Mill Road, it would seem that the world was perfect and everything was as it should be.

CHAPTER TWO

La Vie sans Paris

Grandfather never went to Paris.
Never read Claudine à l'école.
Ne sais pas un Baudelaire d'un Prévert,
Un Goncourt d'un Governeur-général,
and lived to tell the tale.

C lara Malraux's autobiography begins with the words: "In our adolescent world, there was Claudel and Gide, Morand and Giraudoux, Picasso, Gris and Chagall." In this way, through the writers and artists of France, she begins to evoke what it was like to grow up in a bourgeois household in France in the early part of the twentieth century. Writers and artists were the people who passed on the stories and sense of national place. Is is hard to imagine France being France without Victor Hugo and *Les Miserables* or Pagnol's *Le Château de Ma Mère*. Through the stories of writers, Clara Malraux and millions of other young French children gradually took on their own sense of identity, history and nationality.

It was not like this in Acadie. Very recently, there has been a wonderful flowering of Acadian literature and important authors like Antoine Maillet have emerged—but this is all brand new. My grandfather did not read or write. One of the first jobs my father ever had was writing letters for the older generation to friends and relatives in other parts of the country. One of his clients, a fisherman known for his wit, wisdom and skill, always concluded with the words "Please excuse my poor grammar and shaky handwriting," which he obliged my father to write.

Acadie has been a culture without a literature for more than three hundred years. There were no books in my grandfather's house. I grew up without reading a single book about Acadie. There is an Acadian saying, *"un pays se porte dans la bouche"* (a country carries itself in the mouth). This is the way all cultures which do not have writing are passed on. The great empire of the Incas was this kind of culture. Most African peoples have been. (Consider the African saying: "a library is lost when an elder dies.") This is how it was for me. My library was my grandfather. He was born before the Second Métis War in 1885, was a foreman on the first government road around the Cabot Trail, and would die after the first man had walked on the moon.

The stories he told. The way he talked. The many things he could do with his hands. Grandfather did not need the modern world. He could have prospered in eighteenth-century Acadie. He knew how to create a life with not much more than an axe, a drill, a saw and a hammer. The roofs of our house and barn were all pegged together. There wasn't a nail in the place.

The history in books that gives dates and names and battles I learned much later, long after grandfather had gone, but I first learned about the deportation from him. He could remember when there were homes in the steep little valley behind the village. They were built in this rough, inaccessible place because it was hidden from any warship that patrolled the coastline looking for "illegal" settlements of Acadians.

He told me that the stream called "le ruisseau de Paul Doucet" in Chéticamp was named after the same Paul-Marie Doucet who had escaped the deportation at Beaubassin, and that from Paul Doucet's three sons, we were descended. He said nothing more that I can remember about the deportation but that was enough. His words remained more vivid than anything that I would later read in books.

It was common knowledge that our ancestors had ended up on Cape Breton Island because of the war between the English and the French, but the details were mercifully vague. For me, the image my English grandfather Oliver—whom I loved and admired—dispossessing my French grandfather—whom I adored—was tremendously upsetting. This was no fanciful image: my mother had a painting of Grandfather Oliver in the full regalia of the King's Household Cavalry, which he had served in for four years of World War One. It was not much of a stretch for me to imagine my great-great-grandfather Oliver in a red coat exiling my great-great grandfather Doucet from his farm. This wrenching image became part of me, then and now.

It would be years before I would explore exactly what had transpired, for the history of Canada we learned at school was about the English elites of Upper Canada, the French elites of Lower Canada and their various accommodations. The stories of other peoples like the Métis and Acadians became footnotes at the bottom of the page, despite their being older and more complex histories.

The Acadian story begins with a name and an Italian explorer. In 1524, Giovanni Verrazzano crossed the Atlantic Ocean and sailed along the North American seaboard from Florida to Cape Breton. Verrazzano found the coastline of this new world extraordinarily beautiful, and he was moved to call it Arcadia, after Greek legends about a land of wealth and mythic harmony.

A series of European explorers followed, commissioned by various European monarchs. Jacques Cartier travelled up the estuary of the St. Lawrence River for François I of France. Sir Humphrey Gilbert followed, "discovering" Newfoundland for the English court; Hernando de Soto explored South America and the Carribbean for the king of Spain. All had similar instructions: travel, discover, conquer.

The coastline that Verrazzano sailed along was quickly subdivided into distant pieces of royal real estate: Nouvelle France in the north, New England in the middle, and Santa Domingo in the south. It was a time of violent change. Millions of native North Americans died from European diseases like smallpox, influenza, and the common cold, against which they had no defence. Those who did survive the European diseases were quickly driven into remote areas by a long series of wars. For native nations, gross exploitation and genocide were the principal effects of the European dictum to travel, discover, and conquer.

From the Cherokee in the southeast to the Sioux in the northwest to the Métis in Canada, the native peoples were attacked, harried and harassed into inhospitable corners. Where the native peoples had nowhere else to go, as in Newfoundland, Tasmania, and the Caribbean Islands, they were exterminated.

In Europe, Verrazzano's Arcadia came to be known as Acadia or Acadie, although in the New World, it was more frequently referred to as Cadie, which is the Mi'kmaw word for "place." Whether the first settlers shortened "Acadie" to "Cadie" or adopted the Mi'kmaw word is not known, but the new French settlers began to call their new home "Cadie," and themselves "Cagiens" (in Mi'kmaq, "people of the place"). Over time, the Old and New World usages intersected, and both words became commonly used. Cadgiens were known as Acadians, and Acadians as Cadgiens.

The Acadians would be the first non-native people to have a distinctive North American name and culture separate from their European origins. Around what is now called the Bay of Fundy, they created a unique society, an independent blend of European and aboriginal cultures. And like Indian territories, the precise boundaries of Acadie were never exactly defined, though the centre of Acadie was always clear—it was the great saltwater marshes that circled the Bay of Fundy and are now on the border of the present-day Canadian provinces of Nova Scotia and New Brunswick.

The first physical settlement of Acadie began four centuries ago, first in 1604 on the Isle St. Croix in the Bay of Fundy, then, after a disastrous, scurvy-ridden winter on the island, in the spring of 1605 at Port-Royal. Never to be abandoned, this new settlement would grow very slowly. Unlike other European colonies, the Acadian colony did not have large influxes of immigrants. In all, there were only seventy-two families, and they formed, with Mi'kmaw marriages, the entire society.

It was not an aggressive society. They created no military alliances with First Nations peoples, as Samuel de Champlain did in New France. It was a society of settlers, preoccupied with creating farms, hamlets, and villages that could be sustained in a comfortable, peaceful and independent way. The contests between the European royal courts for possession of the entire continent held little interest for these settlers.

The economic strength of the Acadian communities became anchored not in exploiting the vast forests, which abutted the coastline and later would attract colonists into the timber trade to help the British navy construct its immense fleets, but in the invention of a complex system of saltwater dykes.

The dykes operated with swinging gates called clapets that permitted the fresh water to exit when the tide receded, but closed automatically when the tide rose against them. Over a period of 150 years, the construction of these dykes or *aboiteaux*, with their swinging gates, gradually converted the vast, saltwater marshes around the Bay of Fundy into very, rich agricultural lands. At their peak, the dykes were the most extensive in the world. The climate, which was temperate with mild, snowy winters, permitted the cultivation of an exceptional variety of crops, and there was so much arable land it was not all useable by the population.

Without the slash-and-burn forest cultivation that was typical of both the New England and New France colonies, the Acadians made a good fit with the Mi'kmaq, with whom they had neighbourly and trading connections. The Mi'kmaq remained people of the forests and the Acadians people of the shore, and there were no Acadian-Mi'kmaw wars. There weren't even violent incidents. In this way, the Acadians were unique in the New World.

The most familiar part of the Acadian story has always been the deportation, in part because of its dramatic and fatal nature, in part because of Henry Wadsworth Longfellow's famous poem *Evangeline*, which tells the story of two lovers separated by the Grand Dérangement (the great upheaval) of 1755. But the deportation was something that came relatively late to the Acadian colonies. By 1755, they had been established for 150 years and had witnessed years of violence: persistent raids from Boston and constant hostilities between the French and the English. Letters of mark allowed men like Sam Argyle to go looting in the name of liberating the Acadian shore regardless of whether there was any formal declaration of war. But by far the worst violence that the Acadian colonies suffered was a civil war fought between two French aristocrats.

The spark for this war was the death of a single man, the leader of the 1632 expedition, Isaac de Razilly. He died unexpectedly in 1635 just as he was completing his second year in the New World. De Razilly was exactly what the small, struggling colony had needed to grow from a collection of isolated, coastal hamlets into a vibrant community on an equal footing with the other European colonies. By character and connections, Isaac de Razilly was postioned to become the founding genius of Acadie, as Samuel de Champlain would be for Quebec. As a cousin to Cardinal Richelieu, he had what a French governor in the New World required above all: unquestioned support from the highly centralized court of France. Without that support, colonial efforts were easily crippled by the machinations of distant court intrigue. Bastille letters of cachet could follow quickly on the heels of royal patent letters affirming appointment as the king's agent in Acadie.

Fortunately, de Razilly was a natural leader who used his position in society to govern wisely and humanely. He was not a young man just starting out, anxious to prove his mettle to anyone who threatened to test him. He had proven himself long ago, capturing thirty English ships in the naval action of La Rochelle, where he lost an eye, and leading five expeditions against Barbary pirates— all of them successful. And he had a talent for civil administration as well, having created Cardinal Richelieu's colonial policy with his Memorandum on Navigation. Most surprisingly of all, in spite of his military background, de Razilly's notions of how relations should be conducted between people were remarkably free of bellicosity. His instructions to his partners in Acadie regarding the Mi'kmaq were simple and to the point: they were to be treated at all times with "courtesy and respect."

Isaac de Razilly's two years as governor were marked by peaceful relations between all parties, including younger, more impetuous men like Charles de Menou d'Aulnay and Charles de La Tour. The future looked bright. He appears to have spent these two years assessing the needs of the colony, before heading back to Europe to procure the provisions and settlers needed to expand the settlement. He visited Nicolas Denys, a merchant with a long and successful history in Acadie, at his new lumbering operation at La Have (now Liverpool, Nova Scotia). Denys describes this visit vividly in his memoirs. The simple pleasure of the encounter between these two competent and amiable men is evident in Denys' memoir. They held a great feast on long trestle tables, the late summer sun dappling through the trees, a scene reminiscent of the Puritans' thanksgiving dinner in Boston.

As for his relations with New England, Razilly was preoccupied with the Acadian colony, not beating the drums of war. He made no provocative statements and engaged in no military actions with the new English colony. It was clear that he was feeling his way, looking for the combination of strength and civility that could form the basis of future cordial relations. His sudden death at forty-eight years of age arrested his plans for provisioning the colony. And sadly, there was no one of his character, stature, or connections capable of replacing him.

With de Razilly suddenly gone, Cardinal Richelieu made a fatal decision. Unable to choose between d'Aulnay and La Tour, he decided that the governance of the colony was best shared between two governors. With one governor monitoring the other, he reasoned, the Crown would not be cheated of taxes on commerce generated by the new colony. Thus, he separated Acadie into two parts, with d'Aulnay appointed to govern the Nova Scotia side, and Charles de La Tour the New Brunswick side.

This arrangment led immediately to aggressive competition between the two men, but not the kind that produces more revenue for the Crown. Instead, each was suspicious about which side of the line the other's fish, furs, and timber came from. Trading loyalties with the Mi'kmaq were undermined as one side accused the other of buying favours, and the partnership quickly degenerated into a vicious personal squabble. D'Aulnay regarded La Tour as a jumped-up, untrustworthy, *nouveau riche*, whose father had bought his fancy name, and La Tour regarded d'Aulnay as a brittle, antiquated, choleric snob.

Regardless of the cardinal's wishes, a war for control of Acadie ensued between the two men. Nicolas Denys was the first to feel the lash of d'Aulnay's temper. His license to export finished lumber was revoked by d'Aulnay and his foreman thrown into prison at Port-Royal with fifty-pound balls attached to his legs, where he was abandoned to expire in complete wretchedness.

Nicolas Denys was an easy-going, competent man with a gift for building both friendships and commercial operations. His mills at the time of d'Aulnay's attack held more than 20,000 *livres* of stacked, finished wood. D'Aulnay burned all three of Denys' mill yards. Ruined, Denys was obliged to return to France, where he wrote his memoirs and predicted correctly that the envy of the French among themselves would be the ruin of Acadie.

D'Aulnay's father was a royal councillor and distant relative of Cardinal Richelieu, the most powerful man in France. D'Aulnay did not trust or respect anyone not related to him. La Tour was from a different social class, and his second wife was a Huguenot. Not surprisingly, Charles and his father, Claude, had friendly relations with the Huguenot merchants at La Rochelle, who controlled much of the trade and provisioning of France's New World colonies. Unlike D'Aulnay, La Tour had grown up in Acadie. His first wife had been Mi'kmaq and he spoke the language. He knew the land. He was a man who made friends easily.

Together, both men could have become a powerful force for the young colony; D'Aulnay with his connections to Richelieu and Versailles, La Tour with bourgeois connections in La Rochelle to men who knew how to make trade work. Together, they would have made an unbeatable team. In competition, they were perfectly positioned to destroy each other, each having strengths the other lacked. The war between them tore the young colony apart. While Samuel de Champlain built his colony at Quebec and Governor Winthrope built his powerful young colony at Boston, La Tour and d'Aulnay burned each other's trading posts, lumber mills, and settlements, and imprisoned and murdered each other's supporters. No one escaped.

Both men risked many Atlantic crossings to solicit royal preference, financial backing, and new settlers. The vigour and creative attacks of both men succeeded in keeping the other off balance and struggling. It took eleven years for the familial money and court connections of d'Aulnay to finally overpower La Tour's charm and Protestant connections. At enormous personal cost, d'Aulnay rented Le Grand Cardinal, a two-hundred-ton ship bearing sixteen cannons. This ship blockaded Fort La Tour for months. At this time, Charles de La Tour was in Boston trying to convince the colonists there to assist him, but ultimately he was unable to persuade the cautious Puritans to come to the aid of his wife, Françoise Marie Jaquelin, and his supporters, who were trapped in his fort by d'Aulnay's blockade.

The final siege of Fort La Tour lasted through the winter, slowly wearing down both defenders and beseigers. Françoise, with her

Huguenot sympathies, and the three Recollets priests argued. After discovering that La Tour's men had not been paid, d'Aulnay convinced the three priests and a few other defenders to desert. After several more months, the walls of the fort were breached in an early-morning assault, and the long war ended. D'Aulnay, infuriated by the small size of the garrison and the trials he had endured to win it, forced Françoise Jaquelin to watch as he had all the defendants hanged. Françoise Jaquelin died a few weeks later under cir-

> *D'Aulnay, infuriated by the small size of the garrison and the trials he had endured to win it, forced Françoise Jaquelin to watch as he had all the defendants hanged.*

cumstances which were never clear, and Paris newspaper illustrations depicting her at the fort barricades made her a heroine in France.

The d'Aulnay–La Tour war destroyed Acadie in many ways: the eleven years of conflict left the young colony with more ruins than settlements. The population had declined instead of expanded.

Many of the most imaginative, creative settlers were killed or went back to France in despair. D'Aulnay exhausted his considerable fortune on renting ships and soldiers instead of using it to develop Acadie. At the end, Charles de La Tour—his connections to the French court severed, his wife dead, his supporters dead or exiled—fled to Quebec, leaving d'Aulnay the governor a much-ruined Acadie.

Four years later, in 1650, d'Aulnay died in a canoeing accident near Port-Royal as he was searching out sites for new dykes. La Tour returned after this unexpected turn of events and healed the bad blood between the two families by marrying d'Aulnay's widow, Jeanne Motin. Their union seems to have been a happy one, but Charles de La Tour no longer pursued the growth and expansion of the colony. He made no effort to restore the dilapidated fort at Port-Royal or to re-establish himself militarily. Captain Germain Doucet, d'Aulnay's second-in-command, remained the commander at Port-Royal.

When the English attacked and captured Port-Royal in 1654, Charles de La Tour was not on the ramparts or even in the village. He left Germain Doucet, the guardian of d'Aulnay's children, to fight on alone. The captain defended the fort for ten days with what little was left of the French garrison, but, outnumbered five to one, he accepted the inevitable and raised the white flag to negotiate.

If Acadie had been able to prosper and grow between the time of Isaac de Razilly's arrival in 1632 and the English attack in 1654, the Bostonians would have faced a very different community than a hundred tired soldiers and one broken-down fort. The long, debilitating war between the two had weakened the French to the point where they had little left to defend. The terms of the surrender were for the garrison to disarm and stay on in Acadie as private citizens or return to France with their arms.

Germain Doucet decided to return to France with his flags, arms and men, to prepare to fight another day. Exactly what happened to Captain Germain Doucet is not known: he disappeared back into the old continent. I can imagine him walking behind a flag, a single drum beating, as his men follow with their guns at the shoulder marching for a final time down to the bay and to the ship that will take them back to France. But whatever his thoughts about future battles, it must have been a sad day for him, because by 1654, Germain Doucet had spent most of his adult life fighting in Acadie, first for his mentor, Charles de Menou d'Aulnay, against the Bostonians, and then against Charles de La Tour, then on his own as the guardian of d'Aulnay's children.

History has a way of playing tricks on its subjects. Motin and La Tour had five children together, children who married and had large families of their own—as did the two children of Captain Germain Doucet. The descendants of the old enemies would become friends, lovers, and the *porteurs* of Acadie. Charles de Menou d'Aulnay, on the other hand, would have no direct descendants, despite the fact that he fathered eight sons.

For those who stayed, the defeat of 1654 marked a good moment. The ties with the *ancien regime* were finally severed, never again to be restored. The fall of Port-Royal in 1654 (not the initial settlement in 1604) marks the beginning of Acadie as an independent place and the Acadians as an independent people. The departure of the last royal troops allowed those who remained to finally shake themselves loose from the European alliances.

The war between the French and English courts would go on, with great sea and land battles waged around the fortress at Louisbourg on Isle Royale (Cape Breton). But the Acadians kept out of these battles. No new leader like d'Aulnay or de La Tour emerged from the community. Nor were there any elite orders of Jesuits or Recollets sent from France to animate religious and imperial ambitions, as happened in Quebec. Acadie became a forgotten backwater.

The Acadians traded successfully with New England, but relations remained at the level of family businesses. There was no Acadian equivalent to the Hudson Bay Company or a compagnie d'Acadie trading under royal charters, funneling profits back to European shareholders, instead the Acadians did their own trading under their own authority.

On the world scale, the vicious little civil war between D'Aulnay and de la Tour was nothing more than the faintest echo of the great struggles for power that wracked France, England and Germany in far larger, bloodier conflicts. But this war between two fellow countrymen and co-religionists not only destroyed the settlements and commerce of Acadie, it also marked the psyche of its survivors. Between 1654 and 1713, Acadie would change hands between the French and English nine times, but it was a struggle that saw little Acadian participation. After 1654, they left the battles to others. After the Treaty of Utrecht in 1713, Acadian deputies declared formally to both English and French authorities what had already become their practice: they did not want to bear arms for any side.

While they could not have known that the Treaty of Utrecht would mark the last time their homeland would change hands, it didn't much matter. By then their commitment to neutrality had endured for several generations. This was not welcome news for either imperial side, as both regarded the Acadians as subjects—the English because the Acadians were residents of what they considered British territory, the French because they spoke French and were Catholic.

Looking back, the most astonishing thing was not the violence of the Seven Years' War between the French and the English and its many battles, but how resolutely the Acadians behaved. They acted like a sovereign, democratic people, at a time when sovereignty was vested in a feudal tradition of private allegiances based on kinship. The Acadians were the first Europeans in the New World to reject the feudal notion of fealty; instead they governed themselves via village assemblies. While respecting the international authority of larger powers, they considered themselves to be a sovereign, democratic people capable of negotiating their own local, political destiny. This is a complex idea of power sharing that is still not readily accepted by many nation states even at the beginning of the twenty-first century.

Admiral Cornwallis, when presented with this position by Acadian deputies, was so *bouche bée* (astonished) that all he could do in reply was to repeat in a kind of baffled amazement that, "they wanted to treat with the king as if they were his equal!" In the eighteenth century, no one did that, not prime ministers, lords of the fleet or dukes and generals of the army. Not surprisingly, the idea that illiterate peasant farmers might take this position appeared absurd to Lord Cornwallis.

This is not to say the Acadian political position was a simplistic one, for the Acadians did not contest the king's right to include Acadie among his territories. Nor did they dispute his rights to impose taxes or their obligation to pay them, supply his armies with provisions, or billet troops in their homes and villages. They accepted all of these impositions as part of the international order they were subject to. However, they did insist that a wide range of individual and local rights remain vested in the people. These included property rights, freedom of worship, freedom of speech, freedom to govern their own communities in local matters via public assembly, including the freedom to choose not to bear arms, and the freedom to be neutral in someone else's war.

It was this last right that became the sticking point. Everything else could have been negotiated, but not military neutrality. The Acadian insistence on military neutrality would be referred to, in modern parlance, as a "deal breaker."

Acadian neutrality was tolerated between 1713 and 1755 because the British authorities had no choice. The Acadians were too far-flung and the British had too few troops to force them to bear arms. Thus, without any kind of armed insurrection, the quiet Acadian refusal to participate carried the day. After 1713, the Acadians became known as the "neutral french" or "les français neuters," by both the New Englanders and the Canadiens in New France.

This military neutrality was extended to the Acadians' Mi'kmaw and Maliseet neighbours, while in New England, the war between the Europeans and the aboriginal people was of such ferocity it could be described as genocidal. Famous New England "Indian fighters" routinely killed Indian hunting parties, burning and looting villages when they they found them. And for their part, Mohawk, Maliseet, and Mi'kmaw war parties burnt settlers' homes, killed those who defended them, and carried off children for adoption. None of this happened in Acadie.

Today, Acadie exists on no modern map. Its history ended in 1755 when the British could no longer tolerate the Acadians' military neutrality. Acadian villages and farms were "disappeared." Everything that the Acadians could not carry away with them was appropriated by the authorities or destroyed. The villages along the seaboard were burnt to the ground—churches, barns, and houses destroyed. Only the dykes were left standing. The population was scattered down the coast of America from Boston to Louisiana, across the ocean to Europe, and as far south as the Falkland Islands.

When the new settlers arrived from Germany, New England, Scotland, and England, they would find wheelbarrows on the shore filled with rotting clothes and other small items that the deported Acadians were forced to leave behind.

CHAPTER THREE

From a Window

If I could have talked to the sisters of Gerard à
  Lévis,
I would have invited them out on a summer
  night
to the dance in Chéticamp.
When the sun had gone down
behind the mountains,
we would have walked down the road between
  the glistening pines.
The sound of the dance spilling towards us,
spirit, soul and feet ready to float in the beat of
  heaven.
We would have gone to the ocean, swam,
lay on the sand and watched the salt drying
in lace lines on our brown skins.
Felt the bite of the sea urchin
come to rest by our feet.
We would remember that summer forever
in the long echo of our youth.

The bedrooms in our house were all named after my aunts and uncles. The bedroom opposite mine was Aunt Bernadette's, although it had been many years since she had slept there. She had married an Acadian from Maine and lived there, busy with raising her own children. The bedroom next to hers was Aunt Germaine's, where she still slept. The one at the end of the hall was "the boys'," which meant it had been part of the dormitory where the older boys, Alex, Gerard, Denis, Arthur, and Joe, had slept. Now it was a storage room. The room that the younger boys, Armand, Philias, and Fernand, my father, had slept in became "my" room.

Each bedroom had its own history and its own stories. Uncle Gerard had once come home from the woods late at night with a bad injury. Not wanting to wake anyone, he crawled into his familiar bed with his arm bandaged roughly. In the morning, there was blood everywhere and fire in my grandmother's eyes. Why had Gerard not woken someone up and had his arm tended to? She scolded him.

The house was full of these old stories, and they creaked about in corners, waiting to be discovered. One day, I found a beautiful wooden cradle with perfectly spooled sides hanging in the attic under the eaves. It seemed to glow in the half light of the old room. I took it down and brought it to the kitchen to show Grandfather. He looked at it as if it were a ghost, tracing his hands over the delicate spools, say-

Arsène was known for his talents as a carpenter and had built among other things the first merry-go-round in the village.

ing, "Well, well, well," which is what he always said when he was having a conversation with himself.

It was the cradle Arsène Doucet, my great-grandfather, had made for his youngest child, my grandfather's half sister. Arsène was known for his talents as a carpenter and had built among other things the first merry-go-round in the village. When Arsène

drowned in a sudden storm at sea, Grandfather was working in the coal mines in Inverness. Grandfather was twenty and saving money from the coal mine to go west with his buddy to buy a prairie farm. Instead, he was obliged to come home and take over the little farm he had suddenly inherited. Arsène's unexpected death had left four children, counting my grandfather, and a very young second wife, who had had a nervous breakdown after her husband died, leaving her unable to care for the infant—or anyone else. So, at twenty, Grandfather had to take care of his two teenage sisters and run the farm. The infant girl was sent to live with a family in Chéticamp. It was at that time that Grandfather hung the cradle away, high in the attic, and he had not seen it since.

"Well, well, well," said Grandfather, as he rocked the little cradle on the floor. His big hands were knotted like the roots of an old tree and the cradle was like a little boat in his hands.

"What was her name?" I asked.

"Florence," said Grandfather. "She lives in Boston, now."

From my bedroom window, I could catch the first light of the morning as it rose behind the mountains, and the setting sun as it sank behind the sea. From my window, Ulric à Arthur's place seemed to be balanced right on the edge of the sea, while Gerard à Levis' farm was in the other direction, high up, toward the mountains and scarcely visible from the window, so folded into the land were the buildings.

Gerard's father, Levis had one of our horses on permanent loan. At one time, Grandfather had four horses, two stallions and two mares. The stallions were Prince, an enormously muscled black Percheron, and Donald, a tall Hackney-Clydsdale cross. Prince was the strongest horse Grandfather had ever owned—just hitching him up could be difficult. One time, when Prince and Jess, Grandfather's tallest and strongest mare, were teamed up together, he pulled her right off her feet. Prince was much in demand throughout the county as a sire, but he was also mean tempered and Grandfather was obliged to keep him muzzled.

When Donald matured into a tall, fast, handsome stallion with a sweet disposition, so gentle that a toddler could walk safely under his belly, Grandfather decided Donald could replace Prince, and so he became the farm and the village stallion. But Grandfather's little farm no longer needed four horses, it didn't even need two, so Donald was given to Gerard's father, on the understanding that when he needed a team, Grandfather could borrow the stallion back. Even as an old horse, Donald was impressive, with a tall chestnut body and a long stride. He was naturally fast and when driven in a team, even as an old fellow, he would always be a step ahead of his mate.

Gerard à Levis, Grandfather, a hired hand and I cut and harvested the hay for the farm. I suppose we made a strange crew—an old man, two old horses, two young boys, and whomever Grandfather could hire to help him fork the hay onto the truck. Gerard and I were strong and agile. We could secure the hay on the truck, drive the hay rake, and build little haystacks (les meules), but we weren't strong enough to spend the day pitch-forking the hay over our heads onto the truck. That took a grown man's strength. The great confidence that Ulric and my cousin Roland exuded was always a little intimidating; still, Gerard and I were a good team, we just fitted together, and whenever he was there the day zoomed by. I was always in a hurry to tell Gerard some new thought, to see what his reaction would be; from that I would be able to gauge its worth. Gerard à Levis grew into a tall, strong, laconic man with the same wicked smile at fifty that I remember from when I first saw him walking across the field to our house.

Ulric, Gerard à Levis and I were the three musketeers. If there had been a king and court in the distance, we would have saddled up our old farm horses just like D'Artagnan and ridden off to find our fame and fortune. We used to dance on the barn floor, imagining we were Louisiana Cajuns or acrobatic Cossacks home from the Russian wars. Three Acadian boys, feet flying, shouts, stamps, slaps of hands against legs, imagining ourselves grown up, surrounded by more than the soft, violet eyes of curious cows.

Gerard à Levis and I were gangly boys—like young colts, all arms and legs—but Ulric was different. His complexion was clear and soft, always a little tanned. He was fine boned and graceful, with a smile that revealed pearly teeth. Dance came as naturally as breathing to him. He heard the notes and his feet moved.

After high school, Ulric moved to Halifax, but found the city not to his liking. There were ambulances at night, houses stapled side by side, water birds with clipped wings, the cruelty of people sheathed in the comings and goings of invisible Halifax moments. It was a difficult place to be, so Ulric came home to spend his time working at this and that, talking with friends, playing about and looking out through kitchen windows, the kind of windows from which you can see sunlight illuminate the sea ice against the shore.

In a little village, there is not always a place for everyone. I wanted to be a farmer like my grandfather, but he could not imagine it and would not hear of it. It was the time to go to school, get an education, and work in the city, like my father. Grandfather had good reasons to be wary of life in the village. It was not easy, even for those who didn't farm. Uncle Philias was a teacher and a mechanic. Uncle Alex always had at least three jobs, selling stuff (could be anything), renting summer cabins, driving a taxi. Uncle Gerard ran a little sawmill and hauled stuff (could be anything), and had a little farm. The rest of my uncles had gone to find work in bigger places, and Grandfather assumed that my friends and I would too.

For a while, Gerard left for Toronto, but like Ulric, he could not get the hang of the city. He found it to be too confining. He came home and began to look for something to do, eventually running a small co-op industry fabricating doors and windows. Jobs didn't exactly come looking for you in Grand Étang; you had to find or make your own. Gerard bought the old school, and converted it into two beautiful apartments. He still lives there today, not far from the farm where he grew up.

In the old days, people had created small farms up in the mountains, where the land was more or less free to anyone who could stand the winters there. They were fine places in the summer when the sun shimmered in the fields from dawn 'til dusk and alpine flowers bloomed between the legs of fat, grazing cattle. But it was a different story in the winter, when the wind howled like an angry monster and the cows huddled in the barns. The mountain children had to walk for more than an hour just to get to the closest farm to catch a ride to the village school. These farms took a special kind of person, and gradually, they were abandoned for the easier life closer to the village. The pastures that used to climb to the peaks faded into scrub until there was only the memory of them, and the dark green of the forest went all the way to the summit.

> *These farms took a special kind of person, and gradually, they were abandoned for the easier life closer to the village.*

One day, Ulric, unemployed and in one of his periodic fits of enthusiasm for impractical notions, bought fifty acres of the old mountain pastures for back taxes. Oh, what gossip that caused: *Ulric à Arthur—what a scalliwag! Never a sensible moment.* When

other boys were off at university or settling down to good trades, Ulric was buying useless land, filled with nothing but ranting scrub and black bears looking for berries. Ulric just laughed and worked all summer fencing in the old pasture land right up to the forest line, to keep the wild things out, he said. The next summer, he cleared the bush by hand, working like a slave, cutting and burning, making long columns of smoke in the sky, the sweat streaming from his brow until his leather gloves were soaked. In the evening, deer jumped his fence and came to graze where he had worked. Ulric just watched their delicate heads and great violet eyes. He never bothered to chase them off.

In the fall, he plowed and planted his fifty acres from one end to the other, seeding it with clover. By the husk of the ruined house, he left red currant bushes and tall trumpet flowers. The third summer, Ulric's mountain pasture began to glow like a great emerald on the mountain, as if God's thumbprint had settled down amidst the dark forest. People would look up as they passed by along the "chemin du roi," admiring the way sunlight illuminated the great field, sending sparkles to the sky.

In winter, Ulric worked in the village, doing this and that. In the spring, he bought some bees from an old keeper in Margaree for his mountain clover. At first he did not have much success with them. Wandering bears upset the hives and he got stung more than he ought to. His smooth skin became swollen with the distemper of his bees. *Pauvre Ulric, never a sensible moment*, people said, as they commiserated with his mother. But he learned where to set the hives and how to protect them from marauding bears, and his honey was good—very good. It tasted as I imagine honey once did in Greece when they sang of honey cakes, olive oil, and wine. On Sunday afternoons, people from the village began to drive up to buy some honey and admire the view. Then one day a man from the Co-op came and Ulric signed a contract for his honey, and there was no more need to sell it little by little.

Ulric was almost twenty-seven and people in the village began to forget that they had ever doubted him. Instead they said, *That Ulric, il est smart*, which in Cape Breton means that you know what you're doing and you do it well.

All that I learned as a boy in that village became part of me.

Today, when I wake up, I hear city traffic, not the sound of the sea or the crackle of kindling in the kitchen stove, but the feeling that I had as a young boy in my grandfather's house remains. To see the sun rise, to feel the day unfolding before me has always been important to me. So, in the end, each of us did what we were not supposed to do, the three musketeers stayed in the village, each in their own way.

CHAPTER FOUR

Beaubassin, August 1755

"That your Lands & Tenements,
Cattle of all Kinds and Live Stock of all Sortes
are Forfitted to the Crown with all other your
Effects,
Saving your Money and Household goods
and you your Selves to be removed
from this Province."

—From the deportation order, issued by Governor
Lawrence, and read by Lieutenant Colonel John Winslow,
August 15, 1755, in front of the church at Beaubassin,
prior to the burning of the village and the deportation of
the people.

On August 11, 1755, Beaubassin (not *Evangeline*'s Grand-Pré) was the first village from which the Acadians were exiled. It was the largest Acadian settlement in Acadie, with several thousand farmers and villagers grouped along several river basins or "Beautiful Basin," as it was called. Most of these farms and villages were within a few cannon shots of the French fortress of Beauséjour. The French had chosen this site for the fort because it was on the narrow peninsula that divides Nova Scotia and New Brunswick on the rough boundary between what used to be New France and Acadie. The land here is flat and fertile. The stars arch in a great, dense shed above.

A Jesuit priest called LeLoutre had spent years working the Acadians into a revolutionary fervour against "the Protestants" and the "English." LeLoutre's distaste for Protestants was so vivid that he had the Acadian carpenters burn the great church that they had just spent years building, because he felt it was better if it was burnt by Catholic hands than Protestant hands. In the end, LeLoutre was able to persuade several hundred young French boys to join the French colonel DeVergor in his defence of the fortress, but that was as far as the fervour went. The village elders and heads of household held to their neutrality, gave up their weapons and boats when requested, and never offered any resistance to British requests for civilian support.

But regardless of the extent of Acadian compliance, for Governor Lawrence and Admiral Cornwallis, the problem of the revolutionary nature of the Acadian governance model remained. Small, egalitarian, sovereign societies are rarely allowed to endure, because they cannot be controlled by national and commercial elites; and elites have always driven the human agenda. Feudalism, colonization and now globalization are different manifestations of the same age-old human impulse to control the production of wealth by the many for the advantage of the few.

Governor Lawrence and Admiral Cornwallis understood imme- diately and completely that the Acadians didn't need to carry weapons to be a threat to their established order. The Acadian gov- ernance model was revolutionary just by existing. The feudal model couldn't work if people were allowed the freedom to choose whether or not to fight in the king's wars. The only reasonable response from the Crown was to stamp out such a threat efficient- ly and completely, which of course Admiral Cornwallis and Governor Lawrence proceeded to do.

In the pantheon of man's ugliness, 1755 ranks small. There was no intention to kill, torture, or maim anyone. The deportation ships had adequate supplies of food and water for their human car- goes, as good or better than British soldiers got. Colonel Winslow, the young man from Boston who supervised the deportation at the Acadian villages around Beaubassin, was not insensible to the pain he was causing. Writing to Governor Lawrence, he says: "I am happy to have nothing to do with the expulsion at Annapolis, for there is nothing more desolate than the sight of the sufferings of those unfortunate people and I wish to terminate my task at Minas."

Families with close British connections, like the Robichauds and the d'Entremonts at Port-Royal, were allowed to choose their own destination. Both families chose Massachusetts, where they had business and social connections. Most were not so lucky— about a third of the Acadians would die on the ships or in refugee camps swept by smallpox, typhoid, pneumonia, and dysentery.

Some of the overloaded ships sank at sea, killing all aboard. The reality was that overnight the Acadians went from living in independent, remarkably healthy and prosperous communities to being dependent on the charity of others. Victory became surviving each day.

The truth is worth remembering. Each year is connected to the previous year, so unless one understands what really happened in the past, the present is incomprehensible.

When I was in Louisiana at the World Congress in 1999, I met a Mary Doucet who had grown up in California. She had majored in French at university, though she had no idea that she had any French-speaking heritage. But as Mary's mother lay dying, she told Mary something that she had kept hidden all her life: she was a Cadgien from a poor part of New Orleans. Mary's mother described her life, saying she could remember nothing but poverty, harassment, and unhappiness. Determined to lose her language and blend in as best she could, Mary's mother left New Orleans when she was just a teenager. She kept going until she got to California. Mary had come to the reunion in Louisiana to try and find her relatives.

One can dwell for a long time on misery, for pain is common human coin. The Mi'kmaq suffered more than the Acadians. They were hunted for their lives as well as their property. In a few years, disease and war reduced these handsome people from thirty thousand to a few thousand. Consider this excerpt from a petition by Mi'kmaw chiefs addressed to the governor of Nova Scotia:

> *Good and Honourable Governor, be not offended at what we say… But your people… came and killed many of our tribe and took from us our country. You have taken from us our lands and trees and have destroyed our game. The Moose yards of our fathers, where are they?…You have put ships and steamboats upon the waters and they scare away the fish. You have made dams across the rivers so that the salmon cannot go up and your laws will not permit us to spear them.*
>
> *In old times our wigwams stood in the pleasant places along the sides of the rivers. These places are now taken from us, and we are told to go away. Upon our camping grounds you have built*

towns, and the graves of our fathers are broken by the plow and the harrow. Even the ash and maple are growing scarce. We are told to cut no trees upon the farmer's ground, and the land you have given us is taken away every year...

If you think the chiefs overstate their case, this is what Abraham Gesner, Nova Scotia Indian Commissioner, writes in 1849, a year after the chief's petition:

Almost the whole Micmac population are now vagrants, who wander from place to place, and door to door, seeking alms...They are clad in filthy rags. Necessity often compels them to consume putrid and unwholesome food. The offal of the slaughterhouse is their portion...

These are things we need to remember, for remembering is the first step towards building a world where this kind of treatment of our fellow human beings is not tolerated.

For me, the importance of 1755 is not the misery that ensued from Governor Lawrence's precipitous act, for the world is so composed that it is hard to find any human being without ancestors that have not been abused. Think of the Highland Clearances or the many European ethnic and religious wars that have pitted and continue to pit neighbour against neighbour. The importance of 1755 rests, rather, on why it happened and how the Acadians dealt with it.

They dealt with it not through violence, or revenge, or even the bleat of defeat. Instead, they answered by simply continuing to be a people. They did not allow themselves to be extinguished. Empires come and go with remarkable frequency, but this group of people outlasted them. This is the second Acadian message to the world: a people and their culture, music, language, and religion can continue without national boundaries or wars of domination.

Nonetheless, 1755 forever divides Acadie into two places: the Acadie before 1755 and the one that came after. Prior to 1755, Acadie had a territory, a unique relationship with the Mi'kmaq, a specialized way of farming, a continuous history, closely knit communities, and a democratic organization. After 1755, there was a long refugee period of sheer survival, as Acadians were shuttled from one camp to another. While the new communities that would eventually form in Louisiana and in Atlantic Canada would have many resonances with the old, they would also be different.

The effects of the Seven Years' War and the deportation of 1755 would echo down through the generations, not just on individuals, but also on many societies. Two hundred and fifty years later, the scars of poverty and dispersal remain. The expulsion was a defining act for both the Acadians and the Mi'kmaq. The Mi'kmaq were systematically chased off their traditional hunting grounds. Governor Charles Lawrence offered 30 pounds a head for Mi'kmaw scalps. (A similar practice was in place in the New England settlements.) His Majesty's Proclamation, requesting the harassment of the Mi'kmaw community and scalping of Mi'kmaw men, reads:

For the causes we by and with the advice and consent of His Majesty's Council do hereby authorize and command all officers, civil and military, and all his Majesty's subjects to annoy, destress, take and destroy the Indians inhabiting different parts of this Province, wherever they are found and all such as may be aiding or assisting them, notwithstanding the Proclamation of the 4th of November or any further Proclamation to the contrary and we do hereby promise, by and with the advice and consent of His Majesty's Council, a reward of 30 pounds for every male Indian prisoner above the age of 16 brought in alive. And for a scalp of such male Indian 25 pounds and 25 pounds for every Indian woman or child brought in alive. Such rewards to be paid by the officer commanding and any of His Majesty's forts in this Province immediately on receiving the prisoners or scalps above-mentioned, according to the intent and meaning of this Proclamation given at Halifax this 14th day of May, 1756, on the 29th year of His Majesty's reign.

The brutality and difficulty of that period were not recorded by either the Mi'kmaq or the Acadians, as neither practised the literate arts. There have only been three Acadian letters found prior to 1755 and no such Mi'kmaw writings. Without documentation, and with their society fragmented, Acadians forgot that through marriage, the Mi'kmaq had been family.

There is a cartoon in a seventeenth-century Paris newspaper that caricatures an Acadian as a Frenchmen who had "gone native." The Acadian is dressed like an Indian and carries a bow and arrow. As with most caricatures, there is no doubt some truth to the portrayal. The Acadians hunted and fished as the Mi'kmaq did. The young Acadian men admired the Mi'kmaq and copied their skills, but they also lived in settled, agricultural villages, and focused on farming and fishing. Through intermarriage and trade, many Acadians would have learned the basics of the Mi'kmaw language, but the language of their villages remained French. Still, like the Mi'kmaq, their sense of themselves became rooted in the land, the rhythms of the seasons, and the communities in which they lived, not in feudal class systems or military loyalties.

Almost from the outset, there were religious connections between the two peoples. The Mi'kmaq were the first New World people to adopt Catholicism, but it wasn't the liturgical-canonical vision driven by religious teaching orders like the Jesuits, Recollets and Ursulines that was observed in New France. The Acadians had no resident clergy, so they assumed an easy-going approach to religion, adopting elements of Mi'kmaw spirituality as they saw fit. In short, through their connection with the new land and the new relationships they forged there, the Acadians had become their own people, with a distinct vision of themselves. In 1755, this all blew up.

CHAPTER FIVE

Paul-Marie and Le Grand Dérangement

C'est monsieur l'marié et madam' marié	*It is monsieur the husband and madame the wife*
C'est monsieur, madam' mariés	*It is monsieur and madame married*
Qu'ont pas encor soupé.	*That have not eaten*
Un p'tit moulin sur la rivière,	*A little mill by the river*
Un p'tit moulin pour passer l'eau.	*A little mill to pass water through.*
Le feu sur la mountain, boy run, boy run,	*Fire on the mountain, run boy run*
Le feu sur la mountain, boy run away.	*Fire on the mountain, boy run away*
J'ai vu le loup, le r'nard, le lièvre,	*I have seen the wolf, the fox and the hare*
J'ai vu la grand cité sauter,	*I have seen a great city jump*
J'ai foulé ma couvert,' couvert,' vert.'	*I have pushed away my green blanket*
J'ai foulé ma couvert, couverte aux pieds.	*I have pushed my blanket back to my feet.*
Aouenne, aouenne, aouenne, nippaillon!	*Aouenne, aouenne, aouenne, nippaillon!*
Ah! rescou' tes brillons.	*Ah! rescou' tes brillons.*
Tibounich, nabet, nabette!	*Tibounich, nabet, nabette!*
Tibounich, naba!	*Tibounich, naba!*

The origins of this song, called "L'Escaouette," are unknown. No one knows what it means, why or when it was composed. It is one of those cultural mysteries like the summer parade, Le Tintamarre, which people still know about today and have known about in a continuous way since the deportation. But the deportation severed both Le Tintamarre and "L'Escaouette" from their cultural context, leaving them hanging in the air like broken bits of crockery in the soil of an archeologist's dig.

The military defeat at Port-Royal in 1654, which saw Germain Doucet return with the last of the French soldiers to France, brought much good to Acadie. Liberated from the French military presence, the Bostonnais had no excuse to raid the Acadian coastal communities. The French soldiers were not replaced with British red coats; instead, the British Governor preferred to govern Acadie from the comfort of a Boston residence. This left the Acadians to get on with their lives pretty much as they pleased. It wasn't until the establishment of Halifax in 1749, almost a hundred years later, that the British military began to intrude on the Acadian communities.

It was in this world after 1654, the death of D'Aulnay and the defeat of Germain Doucet that the history of Acadie as a place apart begins. Germain Doucet's son, Pierre, listed in a survey of Port-Royal's population as a mason, married a Mi'kmaw woman. The woman died at a young age, leaving Pierre to raise their only child, a boy. He travelled with his young son to Quebec City. After several years in New France, Pierre returned to Port-Royal, where he met and married Henriette Pelletret, a French woman born in Port-Royal. They would raise a large, second family from which most of the Doucets in North America are descended. My own branch of the Doucet family is descended from Pierre's first marriage.

Pierre Doucet would live into his nineties and see his children, grandchildren, and great-grandchildren move up the coast of the bay, where they helped found prosperous new farming communities at Grand-Pré and Beaubassin. These new villages would outstrip Port-Royal in both population and agricultural development. Pierre died in 1714, a year after the Treaty of Utrecht was signed.

The significance of this treaty would have meant a great deal to Pierre's father, Captain Doucet, who had spent his life fighting over who would possess Acadie, but I cannot imagine it worried Pierre very much. He had lived his adult life and most of his childhood in the New World. His wives and children had all been born there. Any memories and attachments he had to France must have been vague at best, and European treaties like Aix la Chapelle and Utrecht would have seemed so distant as to be scarcely plausible.

The allegiances of Captain Doucet's children, Pierre and Marguerite, are clearly to the new land and their descendants will have no references other than New World ones.

Every culture has its golden years. For the Acadians, those years were between 1713 and 1755, the period of English ascendancy. Their villages and farming communities during this time prospered exceptionally. They had a rate of natal survival that has been matched by only a few modern nations. They

The great new French fortresses of Louisbourg on Cape Breton Island and Beausejour on the edge of the Minas Basin were built by the powers at Versailles at enormous expense to protect France's "possessions" in the New World.

had dyked so much land around the Bay of Fundy that its productivity far outstripped their needs. They provisioned the British military and traded extensively with New England using their own small sailing ships. They accomplished what few ordinary people in Europe had been able to do: master their own destiny, become independent of the great landowners.

This is not *Evangeline* legend or retrospective romance. It was reality, though an insecure one at times, to be sure. The Acadians were a New

World people in a situation similar in ways to that of the Basques on the border between France and Spain—a small people balanced delicately between two powerful and aggressive imperial powers, both capable of annihilating them if they so chose.

The great new French fortresses of Louisbourg on Cape Breton Island and Beausejour on the edge of the Minas Basin were built by the powers at Versailles at enormous expense to protect France's "possessions" in the New World. Louis XIV is reported to have said that he poured so much money into Louisbourg he expected to see the walls of the forteress "rise over the horizon." The irony of this great effort is that these imposing fortresses accomplished exactly the opposite. Like Cuba deciding to stock Soviet intercontinental missiles, the creation of these great fortresses, especially Louisbourg, with its giant walls, cannon, and military, frightened the Bostonians and the British navy into paying a great deal of attention to Acadie. It was suddenly necessary to have a naval and military base in Halifax to counter the French fortress at Louisbourg.

And what if the entire Acadian population of Nova Scotia joined the Mi'kmaq and went to war against the English? This became the animating thought behind Governor Lawrence's residency in Halifax. It was the reason that the British demanded the Acadians give up their rifles and their boats. When they did, it took away both the Acadians' mobility and their ability to be aggressive, but that still wasn't enough. The British simply could not imagine the Acadian communities as anything but a threat to British security.

With a British fleet anchored in the Bay of Fundy and thousands of Boston militia billeted along the Acadian coast, Acadian community leaders finally realized that further resistance was futile, that the long talked about deportation was no idle threat. A delegation of Acadians raced overland to Halifax to tell Governor Lawrence that they had agreed to take the oath and would bear arms on King George's account, but it was too late. The dice had been rolled. Governor Lawrence had both the means to transport them and the troops to enforce compliance. He would proceed.

On August 11, 1755, when the soldiers appeared at the village of Beaubassin, Paul-Marie Doucet was eight years old, but unlike the rest of his family, he wasn't scooped up by the troops from Boston and Britain. One can only speculate why he escaped when no one else in his family did. No written record has been passed on to us. Was he playing with some Mi'kmaw friends? Perhaps they were fishing in a stream far from the village. Perhaps he was asleep under a hayrick.

He could not have been a big boy. Eight summers is just enough to learn your language and the rudiments of family life. His parents' worries must have seemed as distant as a church bell, distant as the ships in the bay. But eventually he would have smelled something. Not the pleasant smell of hearth fire, but something more acrid, something bitter. He would have seen columns of dark smoke rising in the sky. The village was burning.

Did he run towards the fires? Or did he just run away? Perhaps he watched from the shelter of the woods. Perhaps he ran right into the family yard. By then the barn walls would have been buckling and snapping with the heat of the flames as the new hay flared in great sheets of orange flame.

Paul-Marie's family were taken away on ships. Some ended up in refugee camps outside of Nantes, France. His mother and father wouldn't survive the camps. Much later, the brothers and sisters that survived the camps re-settled in Louisiana.

Paul-Marie is my family's link between the Acadie of *Evangeline* and the Acadie of today. It is a very thin link. At eight years old, Paul-Marie would have been old enough to have learned his genealogy. He would have known he was "Paul-Marie à Jean à Jean-Baptiste à Charles à Germain," taking him back six generations to his great-great-great grandfather Germain, the grandson of Captain Germain Doucet from France. But at eight years old, Paul-Marie's life had scarcely begun. The few and fragile memories he had of his village of Beaubassin at the edge of the Tantramar marshes would have been nothing more than a few threads. He might have had a memory of his father and older brothers building a new aboiteaux or the sounds of the great flocks of migrating birds that descended on the marshes each spring and each fall in great, noisy clouds of life.

Twelve years after Paul-Marie's "escape," in 1767, one of his brothers made the following declaration, which can be found in the

Rochette papers, a record of some survivors in Louisiana: "My brother Paul-Marie Doucet, born at Beaubassin in the month of January 1746 is presently living at Miramichi." At the time the statement was given, the Miramichi region of northern New Brunswick was a vast, inaccessible wilderness that most Europeans had not yet successfully penetrated. Many of the Acadians who eluded the deportation ships found safety in hunting camps there and in isolated fishing camps along the Gulf of St. Lawrence shore.

Some Protestant, French-speaking merchants from the islands of Jersey and Guernsey were working these coasts and had formed a firm called Robin, Jones and Whitman to exploit the cod fishery. In the displaced Acadians, they saw an opportunity to recruit fishermen and workers for their coastal fishing operations. Caraquet, New Brunswick, was one of these camps. Chéticamp Point, or le Camp chétif, on Cape Breton Island, was another. These homeless, stateless men and women were useful to the merchants so they pressured the governor in Halifax to allow the Acadians to settle permanently in their camps.

Paul-Marie and his wife Félicité-Michele, who may have been Mi'kmaq, wandered into Chéticamp with their three sons sometime in the 1780s, thirty years after the exile began. Paul-Marie and Félicité-Michele are listed as one of the founding families of Fortune Bay, Prince Edward Island, as well as of Chéticamp, though they never seemed to take hold anywhere.

In the early nineteenth century, a missionary passed through the new Acadian community of Grand Étang, Cape Breton, a few kilometres west of Chéticamp. The missionary conducted a rough census, noting in Grand Étang the family of Simon and Scholastique Doucet, and their ten children. Simon was one of Paul-Marie and Félicité-Michele's sons. His farm was not far from where my father and grandfather were born. All three of their sons, in fact, settled in Chéticamp not far from where their father and mother first stayed at "le ruisseau à Paul Doucet."

The last mention of Paul-Marie and Félicité-Michele places them somewhere in the Magré (the Margaree Valley). It isn't surprising that Paul-Marie couldn't stay put. His first and most compelling set of expectations, the beliefs, kinship circles, geography and community celebrations that gave him focus, definition, and purpose had vanished. There are no physical links between Chéticamp of 1786 and Beaubassin of 1755. Chéticamp did not exist prior to 1770 and the village of Beaubassin did not exist after 1755. They are different places with different cultures. There are no salt marshes in Chéticamp, therefore no dyke farming, and no ties to the Mi'kmaq. Even the ocean is different. It is not the coast of a bay, but the wilder coast of the Atlantic. Chéticamp is a northern fishing village bordered by rough, mountain farms more like the homesteads of Scottish crofters than those of Acadian marsh farmers. Nor are there relatives for either Paul-Marie or Félicité-Michele in Chéticamp. Paul-Marie never sees his parents, brothers, and sisters again. The Acadians who gather at Chéticamp in the 1780s come from all points of the compass. They had no direct familial or community connections, except that they were Acadian.

CHAPTER SIX

Sunday in the Village

Gloria, Paschal time
Gloria in excelsis Deo et in terra pax
homminibus bonae voluntatis.
Laudamus te. Benedicimus te.
Adoramus te. Glorificamus te.
Gratias agimus
tibi propter magnam gloriam tuam.

I am about twelve years old. I am standing in front of a station of the cross in the old church at Grand Étang. The priest has given me ten "Hail Marys" and two "Our Fathers" for my penance. "Hail Mary full of Grace, the Lord is with Thee. Blessed art thou amongst women and blessed is the Fruit of Thy Womb Jesus. Holy Mary, Mother of God, pray for us sinners, now and at the hour of our death. Amen." I am saying them as fast as I can, which is very fast, having invented a technique for speed praying. I start out each prayer clearly with "Hail Mary full of Grace," well articulated, so that God can easily discern my good intentions, before segueing at light speed to "blessedisthefruitofthywomb, Jesus" and then the rest. Cheating at penance is, no doubt, a low thing to do, but I can't seem to help it. I want to go out and play. God doesn't seem to mind, I explain to the empty church, but I'm careful to keep my eyes averted from Jesus, who is getting his back flayed.

What were my sins? I can't remember. Old standbys like being disobedient to my parents weren't available, because my parents weren't there. There was just my grandfather, my aunt and me. "Taking the Lord's name in vain" was handy for a good, basic sin, but outside of the school yard it was not frequent. "Exposing my faith to danger by going to heretical churches or reading heretical books" was difficult, as Grand Étang was Catholic through and through and there were no books in our house. "Had I wilfully entertained impure thoughts?" was difficult for a backward twelve year old, with only vague notions of what impure thoughts might be. Yet, I must have had some sins, because there I was saying Hail Marys in front of Jesus carrying his cross. I wouldn't understand until later that I was in training for sins to come.

The Catholic church of my childhood exists in the sense that people still go to mass on Sunday and the priest still administers the sacraments, but the liturgy and church itself are so changed both in form and circumstance that I cannot recognize them. My generation was the last to see the land farmed with horses and the last to celebrate the mass in Latin. This change was so profound that the memory of those days is hard to believe, as if they are ancient, not recent, history.

In 1958, if a stranger had visited Grand Étang on Sunday morning, he would have found no one home. Everyone who could walk or drive was at church. We didn't take the horse and buggy, because that had gone out of fashion for Sunday conveyance. Uncle Philias drove us in his great boat of a bachelor car that heaved down the laneway like a ship under sail. Grandfather wore his blue suit, white shirt and tie, Aunt Germaine a dress and hat, and myself the one pair of trousers I owned with a crease. At the church, the bells would peal and people would gather outside the front door, talking and waiting for the thunder of God's call to stop—the signal that the ordinary of the mass was about to begin.

Father DeCoste was a fine organist and sometimes he would play between the ending of the bells and the beginning of the mass. The music would crash about the church with the metronome power of the sea as we took our seats. My aunt, who looked forward to this part of the service, would take her seat early and listen quietly by herself. It would be many years before I realized that in educated circles there was a name for this performance played just prior to and after a religious service: it was called a voluntary. I always thought Father DeCoste was just showing off.

I was not distinguished by my piety, but I knew the various stages of the mass so well that I could follow them in perfect harmony without ever paying the slightest attention. The idea that the mass was a great redemptive ritual entirely escaped my youthful conscience. I mostly looked around as if at the theatre with the lights on, checking out who was there and what was going on. My cousin Roland, an altar boy, dispatched his duties with nervy insouciance. Gerard à Levis' sisters were awfully pretty and I found it very easy to look at them over the top of my missal. And, when I could gaze at them no longer without getting into trouble with my aunt, I would watch the golden dust motes rising lazily in the window light, imagining they were angel dust. All the time, I remembered to intone along with the priest and server, *Dominus vobiscum. Et cum spiritu-tuo* (God be with you. And with your spirit).

When the mass changed from Latin to English, I belonged to the group of Catholics who never really recovered from this shift. The English mass never seemed quite right. As a boy I was convinced God could hear us better in Latin and that's what gave us the edge over the Protestants. Even the English word "God" seems ponderous, as if God were some remarkably large person. In Latin, God was more like a verb. The meaning and sound of the word always changing depending on how it was conjugated: *deo, dominie, dominus*. Sometimes I would be so comfortable that propped between my grandfather and my aunt, I would doze off, the mass continuing to flow by me.

Communion was the only part of the mass I didn't like. It was long and shuffling, and my lack of piety surfaced with great force. Communion was supposed to be for the pure of heart and purity was not one of my strong points. Fortunately, I was not alone. Aunt Germaine was one of the stubborn few who rarely took communion herself, and her example often gave me courage to sit tight with a small group of hardened sinners. Post communion was my favourite part because it was short and it signalled the end of mass. Soon people would stream out of the church towards the parking lot, chastened and ready to begin Sunday visiting.

I sometimes had lunch at Roland's house, which was only a few doors away from the church. Afterward, we would play in the yard, lofting the ball up to the sky and chasing it across the stones and grass. Sometimes we would go to the cliff edge and lie in the grass, watching the sea roll in at the base. The steady beat of the waves resonated against the cliff, and it was like feeling the heartbeat of the planet against your chest. At some point, I would wander homeward. On the way, I would stop by at Aunt Julite's for gingerbread cookies. Then, it was over to the home of Gerard à Levis to see what he was up to or, more precisely, what his sisters were up to. Sometimes, just before traversing the end of our lane, I would stop at Ulrich à Arthur Leblanc's to walk on the stilts that his father had made for him. It could take until supper time or longer to travel the mile separating the church and Grandfather's.

Sunday was the day that Grandfather bought his annual tickets for the Irish Sweepstakes with the incontrovertible logic, "if you don't buy a ticket, you can't win." It never occurred to me that gambling and God somehow didn't go together—both endeavours seemed chancy. I once whispered to Grandpa during mass, asking if he ever prayed to win the sweepstakes, because this had occurred to me as a useful thing I might do with my time at church. He began to laugh until everyone in the church was looking at him, until the tears ran down his cheeks and he was obliged to take his spectacles off and clean them with a handkerchief. And then he whispered back that the tickets were nothing more than "la grange à David. You don't pray for la grange à David. There's no point." And then he recovered the serious face that church required. I had no idea what la grange à David was, but, mortified by his laughter, I didn't dare ask anything more. But one day driving to Marguerite Aucoin's to buy some bread, the story popped out.

There had once been a family who had lived at the Cap Le Moyne. They were very poor. Their house was hardly any bigger than their woodshed. They lived from hand to mouth, depending on people's charity as much as their own resourcefulness. The father had no luck. He had worked in the woods, but had had an accident, almost losing his leg. He had bought a cow for his little shed and, two days later, the animal lay down and died. At great cost, he had bought sheep and trucked them to the island pasture, where the stupid animals had panicked and jumped straight off the cliff. They were lucky with children though, and had many, though they could not afford to raise them. As soon as the children were ten or so, they were sent off to be cared for by distant aunts and uncles.

In those days, there were many families in the same situation. One summer, the family's eldest son came back from Boston. He had done very well at something, and on the little piece of land behind his father's house, he began to build an enormous barn. He hired some men to help him and, as it began to take shape, it was clear that it would be a barn of great substance. The frame loomed against the hillside; as the men began to close it in, it was clear that it would be the biggest barn in the entire village. The animals from five farms could have been stabled in it.

The young man painted it dark green with a white trim. With its graceful hip roof sculpted like a ship's bottom upside-down, it was beautiful. People came from miles around to see it.

"Where is it now?" I asked, curious because I could not think of any barn like it in the village.

"Oh, it was torn down years ago," Grandfather said. "They had no land. They could put a cow in it and that was about it. David built it because his father had always wanted a barn instead of their little woodshed and apparently the boy had promised his father when he left for Boston that one day he would return with a fistful

Sometimes the old man could be seen standing in his garden gazing at the barn as if it were a painting.

of money and build him a barn. And he did. The old man never used it, but he could see the barn from the house. Sometimes the old man could be seen standing in his garden gazing at the barn as if it were a painting."

"What happened to David?"

"He went back to Boston and when the old man died, they tore the barn down for the lumber."

"It's a nice story, but what does it have to do with the Irish Sweepstakes?" I asked confused.

"You figure it out for yourself, Clive," was all he said, which was not an unusual way for Grandfather to finish a story. So, sometimes I would sit in church and turn "la grange à David" around in my head, imagining its size, its shape, its shingles glinting in the sun, like some kind of Taj Mahal built in Grand Étang, beautiful and foolish at the same time. Did it mean that dreams sometimes do come true, but never in the way you want them to? Or that the Irish Sweepstakes were a mirage, not to be taken seriously?

Sunday afternoon was the time to visit. People dropped in on each other, drank gallons of tea, ate biscuits, and talked, talked, talked. An Acadian kitchen on Sunday afternoon was like improvisational jazz played at rock volumes. No one told the truth, but no one lied outright either. There were rules.

Wit was the great treasure of Sunday afternoons, and television was of little consequence. In stories there was always fun and for those with ears to hear it, there was also the history of the village. Each person in the story had to be identified; who they were related to and what they had done with their lives was an obligatory context that had to be set down in order to make the story legitimate. Once these details were agreed upon, then anything was fair—no matter how outrageous! Frogs could talk, men could outrun horses, and simpletons had the smartest mouths in two counties:

One day, the priest saw Isaac picking berries by the side of the road. Isaac was what, in those days, would have been called simple, but he was the kind of simple that could be witty, brilliant even. The priest, who liked to tease Isaac, asked him if he'd like a drive down to "la maison des fous," which was the common name for the asylum that hunched like a dark shadow behind the village of Mabou.

The priest didn't scare Isaac for a second. He replied, quick as a wink, "Sure, but who would drive the car back?"

The priest blinked dumbly before he understood, then laughed and laughed until tears ran down his cheeks. The story flew around the parish as if it had wings.

And then there was the eternal question, "Had Moise à Polycarpe caught a fox by the tail?" No one had seen him do it, but then no one had not seen him do it either. Everyone knew that Moise could run like the wind. He could out-run a horse, so why not a fox? Having mulled this over for a moment, people would begin to tell their stories about Moise à Polycarpe, each person trying to top the last.

One day, Lionel Levert came upon Moise à Polycarpe walking along the chemin du roi, driving his father's light buggy with a fast horse and rather proud of it. He stopped and asked if Moise would like a drive. Moise replied, "No thanks, I'm in a hurry."

Sunday was not my day to shine: my French was slow and clumsy, so I spent a lot of time listening. Still, I liked it; I liked the change in the rhythm of the week and I looked forward to it. Sometimes, when it was particularly hot, someone would drive us to the beach in Chéticamp where the sea curled far against a sand bar and the water was salty and warm. Sunday was a comforting day all round. There was something immensely reassuring about the rhythm of the mass and the figure of the priest conducting us down the familiar pathways of prayer, his vestments glowing in the sunlight as it filtered through the stained glass.

In the end, although Sunday was a serious time for prayer, it was a greater time for gossip, which flowed up and down the lanes of the village like an electric current. Who was courting who? Who was sick? Who was having good luck with the fishing? Who was not? Who was drinking too much? Who was visiting from Boston?

During the week, fishermen stitched checkerboard nets to catch the passing fish, and people visited cousins for tea and fricot. Invisible lines were traced back and forth across the village, from house to house, from farm to post office, from house to store, from child to parent, until all were safely gathered in.

CHAPTER SEVEN

The First Butterfly of the Evening

Pendant le crépuscule,
un petit flot de souris-chauves
sort du grenier,
vole dans l'air,
ici et là
mendiant dans le ciel.
Elles ne semblent pas naturelles,
ni oiseaux, ni souris,
même le mot, les souris-chauves
est laid
et je cours vers Grand-maman
certain que les sauvages souris-chauves
peuvent me manger comme le fricot.

(*this poem appears in its entirety on page 115*)

The story of the first butterfly of the evening was told to me by my grandmother. I had just seen my first bat—it had come sweeping out from under the house eaves followed by a small cloud of flittering figures. There was something unnatural in their sudden, jerking flight. Frightened, I ran to my grandmother, who was sitting on the porch catching the last view of the sun's blaze as it settled behind the ocean. How old was I? Old enough to run on my own two feet, but young enough to believe Uncle Philias when he said, "Watch out for bats, they eat little boys." And young enough to be gathered onto my grandmother's lap where, calm and serene, she told me a story I have never forgotten, and one day hope to tell to my own grandchildren.

"Don't worry," she murmured. "Bats bring good luck. They are the butterflies of the evening." I looked up at the sky from the safety of my grandmother's lap. The bats were much larger than butterflies, larger and darker, though they did fly in a similar fashion.

"Would you like to hear the story of the first butterfly of the evening?"

I nodded, still unsettled by their strange silhouettes.

"Once upon a time there was a mouse, the smallest mouse in the field, and all the animals teased him. Even worse, many of them wanted to eat him. Yes, eat him. The foxes would have liked to eat him for a little snack. The crows would have liked to eat him for lunch. The owls would have liked to eat him for both a snack and lunch. The poor little mouse lived a life of flight and fear.

The bats were much larger than butterflies, larger and darker, though they did fly in a similar fashion.

"One day, the little mouse was looking up into the sky, fearfully searching for crows and owls, when he decided suddenly that the solution to all of his troubles was to learn how to fly, like the seag-

ulls and the eagles. In the sky, no one could bother him. He would be free. So each night, when the crows were asleep, when the foxes were quiet, and before the owls had left their trees to go hunting, the little mouse set about teaching himself to fly. He stepped onto a little rock and beat his arms like wings, like the seagulls and the eagles. But each evening he failed to fly. He didn't launch himself into the sky. He remained fastened to the ground, a foolish little mouse in an enormous field.

"After a few evenings of his practice flying, the life of the little mouse became more precarious because the crow noticed his foolishness. Each evening when the little mouse came out of his hole, the crow was waiting for him and the poor little mouse found himself running for the underground, not the air at all. One evening, the crow caught the little mouse in his beak, but the mouse wriggled away, and the crow lost him. Hurt and bleeding and scared near to death, the little mouse hid in his hole once more.

"But, as soon as his hurts had healed, he wanted to try to fly again. Carefully watching the sky for the crow, he tried again, but it was as before: He didn't have the slightest success. The rabbits, the other mice, the birds, the insects, and the cows made fun of him. They all said the same thing: there is a crazy mouse in our field who is almost bald from the crow's attack. They had no sympathy at all. 'Bon Appetit, Master Crow,' they said.

"Master Crow smiled to himself, sure that it was just a matter of days before he dined. The animals in the field were right; it couldn't last. The life of the little mouse would surely finish in the copious belly of Master Crow.

"One evening, God happened to be passing by the field and he noticed this battle between the crow and the little bald mouse. He decided to stop the fight and put Master Crow in one corner and the little mouse in another. Neither was very happy. The mouse was terrified and the crow wanted his dinner. 'Calm yourselves,' said God, 'and tell me what is happening.'

"The little mouse explained to God that he wished to fly like a bird. Master Crow explained that he wanted dinner. When God heard this, he started to laugh. He laughed so hard and so long that he created a wind that pushed the little mouse across the field like a leaf in autumn. The little mouse was so confused and so excited by everything that he began to think that he was flying. He cried out, 'Look, look, I can fly!'

"When God heard this he began to laugh even louder, and the wind grew stronger until the barns and the houses began to shake. Finally, the wind calmed down and the little mouse returned to the ground, half dead with terror and exultation at his adventure.

"God picked up the little mouse in his hand and said very gently, 'You are a very brave little mouse, the bravest that I have ever seen. You have the right to fly like an eagle, but I already have a world full of eagles of every type. There are fish eagles and rabbit eagles and golden eagles and bald eagles. What to do? In fact, the world has more birds than I know what to do with already. There are millions. My fields are filled with them and where the birds are not, the butterflies are. What to do?'

"The sun was then sinking, and the evening twilight was casting shadows across the earth. It was quiet. There were no butterflies or birds about, and suddenly God knew what he could do. He breathed very gently on the little mouse. The mouse sprouted wings and flew off into sky and God said, 'You will be my first butterfly of the evening.' That is how the little mouse grew wings and became the first butterfly of the evening, and was safe ever more from Master Crow."

My grandmother's funeral was the last time the entire house was filled to the rafters, from the dormitories to the bedrooms. She died not long after Father DeCoste. He was sixty-eight and she was seventy-two. In my mind, their deaths mark the end of an era. He died walking from the presbytery to the church. He died between the traces, as we say in Cape Breton, still trying to pull people toward heaven. My grandmother died from a blood clot that would not dissipate in legs that were worn out. The next generation of women would not be like hers—a generation of women to raise enormous families and run farms with their husbands.

All I have of her is this story and the memory of a voice. Yet she was often there in different ways. She was there in the way my uncles spoke of her. She was there in the garden, a little place not far from the house, with flowers along one edge, clots of colour in the summer sun. On Sundays, Grandfather would till it, although it was not his favourite place: he always began the weeding with a litany of complaints. "A garden is for fishermen," he would say, "to give them something to do in the afternoon." He would grumble as he moved slowly up and down the narrow rows of lettuce and beans, carrots and cabbages, hoeing away at the weeds.

His garden was the farm, field tilled in its own way, potato and turnips by the sea cliffs where the earth was deep, apple trees by the pond to catch the sun, hayfields climbing up to the mountains. A garden grows so little—some struggling green lettuce, thin snow peas against the fence, onions and carrots that protest leaving the winter seed for thin soil and the brush of a cool sea wind. It never seemed strange to me that Grandfather tilled what we always considered Grandmother's garden, nor was it strange that we kept it for her.

CHAPTER EIGHT

"What Do You Want, Babe?" New Brunswick, Louisiana, Nova Scotia

Horizons
There is an edge
to a hayfield.
It is the same edge
as the line
between sky and sea
the same taste of eternity.

Soon the third and largest Congrès Mondial Acadien will take place in Nova Scotia. From one end of the province to the other, from my grandfather's little village of Grand Étang to Baie St. Marie and Grand Pré on the Bay of Fundy to Halifax, Acadians will gather to celebrate their culture. When I talk to friends in Nova Scotia, they frequently mention the coming congress. They know it's going to be big because every room and every bed in the province has been booked, but they always refer to it somewhat confusedly: "You know, the big Acadian festival," they say—"the Acadian party, the conference, the family reunion, the birthday—you know what I mean."

They shouldn't feel bad about not quite knowing what it's all about, because most Acadians aren't sure either. For some it is an excuse to track down old friends. For others, it's a chance to party and hear some great music. For others, it's a time to stock up on Acadian books, and attend lectures and seminars on things Acadian. For the historically inclined, it's a birthday celebrating four hundred years of Acadian settlement. For many, it's all about family reunions.

When the idea of a world congress was first proposed by some Acadians from Alberta, the idea was at once so simple that anyone who had been to a family reunion could understand it, but on a scale that no one had ever dreamed of before. To reunite at one time all the Acadian families of the diaspora—from Louisiana to California, from California to British Columbia, from Quebec to France—was a wildly ambitious thing to propose. Initially there was a good deal of resistance to it. The sceptics, however, were proven wrong: the response was bigger and more intense than anyone imagined it would be. Over a quarter of a million people came—more Acadians than live in the province of New Brunswick.

No one had ever seen anything like it before. Five thousand Leblancs came for the Leblanc reunion alone. It was so large it had to be held in a hockey arena with video screens, and the family reunions were just a part of the celebrations. For sixteen days, an Acadia that no one had ever seen before was invented. It was an international place, with theatre, concerts, book fairs, films, poetry, music, art, and conferences, a place where the new priests of Acadia, the academics, gathered to meet, talk, and pontificate. The United Nations decided to designate this first world gathering of Acadians the cultural event of the century. Both UN Secretary-General Boutros Boutros-Ghali and Prime Minister Jean Chrètien came to speak at the opening ceremonies.

But what was it about? I certainly didn't know. I wasn't even sure why I was going. My own branch of the Doucet family had had a reunion in Grand Étang just a year previously. Thus there was little chance I would even meet immediate members of my family.

When I arrived it took me days to figure out how all the events fitted together because reunions, conferences, beach parties, concerts all banged up against each other, overlapping and separated, often by several hundred kilometers. It was all such a jumble, but as the days passed I began to understand that the Congrès Mondial was about creating a mythical place, a place that might have existed but for the fortunes of history—an Acadian city.

For a few weeks, it was normal to walk down any street in the city of Moncton and run into Acadians from different places; businessmen, artists and professors rubbed shoulders with fishermen, farmers and truck drivers. Rock groups had names like 1755 and

Le Grand Dérangement, and no one had to explain what these names meant. French was spoken in all the rainbow accents of the planet. For sixteen days, the Acadian diaspora materialized out of separated families into a shared history, culture, language and place.

I found it overwhelming meeting so many people—Warren Perrin from Louisiana, the lawyer who has been central to the Acadian revival in Louisiana; Antonine Maillet, the author of *La Sagouine*; Barbara Leblanc, the director of the Grand-Pré historical site. Each day, there was a new galaxy of "stars" to meet in the most ordinary and pleasant ways, over a coffee, on the beach, at a barbecue. Many of them I had heard or read about but never expected to meet.

Five years later, I was drawn to the second world congress in Louisiana more by curiosity than anything else. I had never travelled that far south and wondered what Louisiana was like.

I landed in Lafayette, Louisiana on August 1, 1999. It was 98 degrees Fahrenheit when my foot hit the tarmac. The heat was like a blacksmith's hammer against my head. The sun bounced from the pavement, sending white daggers into my eyes. It amazed me that my legs still worked. *This is where my relatives live*, I thought to myself, a little stunned at this idea because my instinct was to get back on the plane and go home.

But the airport was air-conditioned. The rental car was air-conditioned. The hotel was air-conditioned. The restaurants were air-conditioned. It was like the reverse of Canada at 30 degrees below zero. People did not stay outside longer than it took to go from one air-conditioned space to another. I became convinced Spanish moss hung from the trees because it takes less energy to hang from a branch than to grow from the ground.

Louisiana was one long voyage of discovery. To my surprise, the Acadian villages of Louisiana that dot the countryside around Lafayette were more French in their form than the villages of Atlantic Canada. Places like St. Martinville and Abbeyville are built around the classic French square or "place," exactly as countless French villages are built. The church and the Hôtel de Ville are each on one side, and businesses and cafés fill in the two others. These old villages were beautiful, and I found myself staring up at a street sign shimmering in the noon heat. It said "Chemin Doucet." The sign was next to a gas station that said "Leblanc Fuels." It was strange to see such familiar signs so far from home.

The family reunions took place in the villages, as they did in New Brunswick, this time not along the Gulf of St. Lawrence but in an arc along the Gulf of Mexico—all the way to New Orleans. St. Martinville. Abbeyville. Erath. Houma. From the squares of these little villages, it was easy to see how the Cajuns managed to hang onto their language and sense of identity for so long, even in the great American melting pot. Fifty years ago, Cajun Louisiana must have been a necklace of remote tropical places with each village cradled not by malls but a checkerboard of small fertile farms. The farms themselves would have been cut and re-cut by an intricate latticework of creeks and streams. Like Grand Étang, each village must have been a kingdom.

On my first visit to St. Martinville, it took me twenty minutes to get there from Lafayette. On the way back, I decided to take one of the old, local roads. At first, it was fun. I rolled the windows down and drove slowly through the delta farmland. The cicadas made so much noise they seemed capable of flying away with the trees. The smell and feel of the ripening sugar cane settled around the car in a solid green wave. I kept expecting some landmark to emerge out of the night so that I could get my bearings and find the way back to Lafayette. After all, I wasn't far from the city.

It took me some time to realize that no such landmark was going to emerge and that I was lost. I had absolutely no idea where Lafayette was or what direction I was travelling in. I could have been going south toward New Orleans, north toward Baton Rouge or west towards Texas. I could find no road signs, not that they would have helped—the little roads I was on weren't marked on the map anyway.

The night was baking hot, the houses dark. In the little hamlets I occasionally came upon there were no street lights. The houses sat far back from the road, half hidden by spreading trees, dark and humped like stacks of hay. An hour passed as I turned around and around in the delta heat, never seeming to get anywhere and not knowing where I was going. I couldn't decide which was more irritating: the car's air-conditioning, cold and grinding against my body, chilling the car like a meat locker, or the stifling night air. The air was so hot that just breathing made me sweat.

I stopped the car at the edge of the road and looked down a darkened lane toward a large house surrounded by looming trees. One window was softly lit. Was there anyone awake? Examining the map again by the car's cab light, I confirmed what I already knew: that I didn't know where I was.

I got out of the car and stood alone by the edge of the road, uncertain of what to do, certain only that I didn't want to be in the car anymore. Suddenly, a caravan swung by in the night. Inside, a yellow electric light illuminated a woman standing at the sink doing dishes. She was stripped down to a halter top and short, tight jeans. I watched for a moment, and then the caravan, weaving, disappeared around a corner. The yellow light, the homely chore of doing dishes, the long brown arms, how desirable it all seemed. I looked at my own car, which was ugly in comparison, hot and useless. *What am I doing here, driving around lost in the night?* I thought.

I never did develop a sense of how one navigates in the Mississippi Delta, and getting lost in Louisiana was something I would become accustomed to. The next day, I got lost again, this time on my way to the Doucet family reunion in Opselosus. I was on a country road somewhere between Pointe de l'Église and Opselosus, surrounded by a green canyon of sugar cane. The heat covered the road like a hot stone wall that only brute force could push through. I could feel bubbles of panic at the thought of driving around in confused circles as the sun's heat climbed toward the noon climax, frying everything foolish enough to be out and about. Deprived of any illusions that I could find my own way out, I began searching the roadside for anyone who could help me with directions.

I came around a curve and a country store appeared on the right side of the road. It stood alone, surrounded by cane sugar fields. A one-storey, white, clapboard place with a single gas pump outside, it looked like it had been built for a Hollywood movie set in the south. There was no sign of life about the place. The windows were shuttered and a tiny wooden door hung in the front of what looked to be more of a loading dock than a porch. It did not look like the kind of place where some corporate attendant in a polyester uniform jumps out and asks, "How may I help you?"

No one appeared when I pulled up.

This struck me as a good thing. I got out of the car and pushed through the small wooden door. Inside, it was shadowed and cool. There was no air-conditioning, which was fine because I'd come to dislike it. I preferred to sweat. Once inside, I was given the impression of tall, well-stocked shelves, and an ordered, comfortable, clean and well-tended store. Through the gloom, I could make out a wooden counter at the back of the store with someone behind it. I walked quickly toward the counter and the man. Behind the counter was a spotless kitchen with a bright, impeccable linoleum floor. There, a white-haired lady sat in one of two rocking chairs, rocking quietly. It looked vaguely familiar.

I asked for directions to Opselosus. The man, about my age, took a long look at me, regarding what was no doubt my weird attire. Louisiana men do not wear shorts, sandals and golf shirts, not even in one hundred degree heat. Louisiana men with real jobs wear blue jeans and boots, and they look like they can sweat. No doubt about it, I felt self-conscious. On the other hand, I'd be damned if I was going to wear blue jeans at a hundred degrees. I smiled, and—probably because I was feeling cranky—I repeated the request for directions, this time in French.

The man replied immediately in French—the old Acadian French of my grandfather. The accent was as unmistakable as a thumbprint. Once you've heard it, you never forget it. I asked him for his name, which he told me was Aucoin. I introduced myself.

It turned out I wasn't far from the Doucet reunion, but I carefully wrote the directions down anyway. He watched me write, and when I looked up, he was smiling at me and I was smiling back. We both suddenly realized that the only reason that he was on the Louisiana side of the counter and I on the customer side was because of something called the Deportation. Until that moment, I don't think that I had really believed in any visceral way, despite the street signs and the architecture, that there were any Acadians in Louisiana. I thought that it was all stuff for the tourists. These cynical feelings fell away at the sound of the man's voice.

He asked me where I was from and I told him. He shook his head in wonderment. I felt the same way. He asked if I wanted a coffee. I accepted and we talked for a long while. It felt like I had arrived, finally found the reason I had come.

At the Doucet reunion, I met some Doucets from California, Chicago, and Moncton, and a Dugas from St. Martinville. We agreed to meet for dinner that night. It turned into a very merry affair. We couldn't stop talking and laughing. At the table was an amateur genealogist from Moncton, a Creole-Cajun artist named Stephen Dugas from St. Martinville, Mary Doucet-Morgan from California, and me. The conversation ripped around between French and English.

We were all long-lost cousins, all descended from Germain Doucet's children, Pierre and Marguerite. Marguerite married an Abraham Dugas. Stephen, being a Dugas, is a descendant of Marguerite Doucet, which also makes us cousins…four centuries on. I told Stephen I'd always wanted a coloured cousin, my own family being way too vanilla. We laughed. Mary took a photo of us clowning together.

After dinner, we made our way over to the launch of Stephen White's next genealogical tome on Acadian families. Stephen White is not a saint, exactly, but I can't think of any other way to describe him. Everywhere he appeared at the congress, he was surrounded by admiring crowds, his every word followed with the closest attention, because Stephen knows the genealogical trail of Acadian families better than anyone else on the planet.

I had never met him before, and he had never met me, but I felt him to be an old friend because I had come across his name in so many places. *Selon Stephen* (according to Stephen) carries such an imprimatur. Stephen White has done more to unlock the hidden history of Acadie than any other person because it is his genealogical research which has exposed the family history of Acadie. Who married whom, where they lived, and what they did, until a picture of the wanderings of the Acadian people emerged.

I shook his fine-boned academic hand and said with an uncontrollable grin, "I'm Clive Doucet. Do you know where I'm from?" He looked at me for a second and then calmly replied, "One of the Doucets from the Magré (Margaree Valley)."

I said, "Yes," not at all astonished that he could pinpoint within a few kilometers from all the places in Atlantic Canada where my branch of the family had settled. Looking back, I think to myself how insensitive it was to put him on the spot like that.

Stephen White is not alone in his rediscovery of Acadie. Warren Perrin and Zachery Richard in Louisiana have slowly been unraveling the confused history of Acadie, each in his own way. Zachery has done it through his songs and Warren Perrin through the creation of museums, French schools in Louisiana, and a petition to the British crown for recognition of the deportation. The depth and breadth of this long confusion is difficult to convey; for many Cajuns, it resulted in a systematic misunderstanding about their own history. Nothing was ever taught except in fragments of family history and in legend that was more myth than history. Assumptions and speculation—such as that Cajun ancestors were forced from Canada because they were criminals—replaced fact. I thought for years that the *Evangeline* poem was nothing but a romantic fiction, but the more I learn about the history of Acadie, the more it seems like a plausible reflection of reality—even the most outlandish elements.

In Longfellow's poem, Evangeline follows the trail of her Gabriel out onto the American prairie, always just a step behind him, until she loses him completely. I had always thought this was pure fiction. Why would Gabriel wander out into the vast centre of the North American continent? Louisiana, yes, because there was a connection to France. New England, yes, because there had been long-established commercial and trading connections with Acadie. But the unexplored western country of the Indian nations? Surely that was just an imaginary destiny from the mind of the poet.

At a book sale in Louisiana, I come upon a book called *Life Among the Plains Indians in their Final Days of Glory, the first hand account of Prince Maximillian's Expedition up the Missouri River, 1833–34.* What attracted me to the book was not the long, imposing title, but the paintings. Prince Maximillian took an exceptional artist named Karl Bodmer with him; Bodmet produced marvellous, coloured paintings of the Indians and Indian nations they encountered. In Louisiana, I flipped through it admiring the paintings and drawings. I didn't read much of it until I get home, where I discovered it to be a fascinating and absorbing account of the Prince's trip into country only a handful of Europeans had ever traversed. I was about a third of the way through the book when I learned that one of the prince's guides and translators was a man named Doucet. When I first came upon the name, I was so astonished that I almost dropped the heavy book.

What was a Doucet doing in the middle of the American West? In order to be a translator and guide, he must have been born and raised in those territories. Suddenly, Evangeline's long and difficult journey into that landscape didn't look so fanciful. Clearly, some Acadian boys did drift quite far from Nova Scotia, and the proof rests not just in Maximillian's diary, but also in the Doucet name and other Acadian names that can still be found in the American west and among the Métis people of Western Canada.

The Congrès Mondial in Louisiana was full of these unexpected discoveries. Some people, like Jean-Marie Nadeau, I had planned to meet, but meeting others, like a second cousin from Grand Étang who I hadn't seen since I was sixteen, came as a complete surprise. Roger Doucet's father, Calixte, had been the manager of the village co-op. He used to intimidate me a little because he was such a huge man. Roger laughed. "My father was a gentle giant. He wouldn't hurt a fly." We both laughed this time. It was good to see him.

In the St. Martinville town hall, I went to listen to Grand Captain John Joe Sark, Captain of the Micmac Grand Council, talk about Mi'kmaw history and experience. It is a long history and, until the arrival of the Europeans, an immensely successful one. For at least ten thousand years, the Mi'kmaq were the dominant people in the territory now composed of the Gaspesie, the state of Maine, and all three Canadian Maritime Provinces. Not surprisingly, the Mi'kmaq were the first to cross paths with the Europeans. They had been summer trading with Basque fishermen for centuries, though no one knows for quite how long, because the Basque had been very good at keeping secret the rich fishing grounds off Newfoundland from European competitors. When the first French explorers and settlers arrived, they fitted into this long established trading pattern with the Mi'kmaq.

Chief Sark explained to those who didn't know the story that it was a different experience in the Dutch, British and Spanish colonies where the native peoples were regarded as enemies and a long war of attrition developed. Initially, the Mi'kmaw people had some successes in this war, and they remain the only native North Americans to defeat the Europeans in a sea battle, using only large canoes.

This vision of the "Indian" in New England as a deadly enemy grew rather than diminished. Plaques to early settlers "murdered" by Indians can still be found in downtown Boston, and although by the time of the deportation the Mi'kmaq had long retreated to Canada and the farthest reaches of Maine, fear of them remained. In 1755, young Colonel John Winslow, all of twenty-four years old, wrote in his diary that he was leaving Boston "on a great project" to deal with the French, who had always encouraged the Indians to "murder us in our sleep." At the time, the American settlements housed a population of over a million people. In contrast, the Acadian population numbered about 13,000 with the Mi'kmaq about the same.

Nonetheless, Colonel Winslow genuinely felt the Mi'kmaq and the Acadians were New England's great and deadly enemies. He was not without his reasons: the Acadian hamlets were never attacked by the Mi'kmaq whereas the English were, and the Acadians refused to commit fully to the British side. It is understandable that these group were, at the very least, not to be trusted.

This long, complicated story of the Mi'kmaq and the Europeans sounded so simple coming from Chief Sark, but it isn't, and like the Acadian story, it is still with us. For the first time, I heard Chief Sark talk of the government residential schools in New Brunswick and their effect on Mi'kmaw culture, language and families. He told the story of Peter Labobe from Lennox Island who ran away from the residential school in Shubenacadie in the dead of winter. Before he was caught, his feet became frostbitten. He received no medical help, his head was shaved, and he was locked in a closet as punishment for running away. His feet became gangrenous and some toes had to be amputated. His teachers used him as an example of what would happen if they tried the same.

The translator, a slight young woman from St. Martinville with a wonderful Acadian accent, began to cry and could not continue. A man from the audience stood up to complete the translation of the story for those who did not understand English.

John Joe Sark spoke simply and with easy warmth. He knew his history, both oral and written. He knew when the New Brunswick government passed the bill permitting the sale of Mi'kmaw lands and when Prince Edward Island was divided into sixty-two lots and sold like so many bales of hay. Mi'kmaw titles did not exist. He explained the Concordat between the pope and the Mi'kmaq from 1610, and the treaty of 1752 between the British Crown and the Mi'kmaq. But by then, the Mi'kmaq were so weakened they were not in a position to insist that their treaty be respected, so it was broken more often than not. He finished his story with a twinkle, and the suggestion that the Acadians and the Mi'kmaq had done more than hold hands. This brought laughter.

My heart was very full and like the translator, I was not far from tears. I remembered that at the first congrès mondial, the Mi'kmaq had not even been invited and I was thinking how I would not be here if I did not have Mi'kmaw grandmothers. I was thinking how wrong all this was. Suddenly, I was on my feet, speaking. It seemed like someone else was speaking, not me, because I had come just to listen, not to say anything.

I said: "We have forgotten our history in Canada. We have forgotten that we have Mi'kmaw grandmothers. We have forgotten that the Mi'kmaq took us in and saved our lives during the deportation. We have forgotten that Mi'kmaw names are written on baptismal certificates as godparents. We have forgotten that many of our ancestors could speak Mi'kmaq, but today I know no one who can even say *bonjour* in Mi'kmaq. We have forgotten all this and many of us have become racist in our forgetting."

And then I sat down and said no more because I was trembling.

There was a sharp, deep silence after I spoke. John Joe Sark did not reply and I began to think that I had offended people. Then a woman from Louisiana stood up to speak. She said that the same thing had happened in Louisiana. The Houma are French-speaking native people who had befriended the Acadians when they first arrived in Louisiana. The woman said that the Houma had not been invited to the reunion in Louisiana until the very last minute—too late for them to come. The Houma had been treated as decorations, instead of people. She sat down, and her voice was trembling also.

In Louisiana, I discovered, there is a fierce underground battle going on against the homogenizing effect of mall culture and the global mantra. The battle lines are drawn around French immersion schools, traditional music, and the fierce desire to remain Cajun. It isn't an equal battle—it is more like a series of forced retreats—but it is a battle which has been engaged nonetheless. Over twenty-two Louisiana parishes now have French immersion schools and everywhere people are struggling to maintain connections to their first language and to the past, through music, through dance, through museums and education.

As in Atlantic Canada, several traditional Acadian villages in Louisiana have been maintained as historic sites and have become places where Acadian theatre, dance and music thrive. I spent an evening in one of these Louisiana villages, watching an Acadian group perform a folk musical about a Cajun wedding set at the turn of the century. In the sweltering heat of an old thrashing floor, the audience clapped and sang along with the dancers. There were no microphones or sound systems, just the sounds of the human voice in the air, human feet on the floor, and the music that could be made by an accordion, a washboard, a fiddle, and assorted spoons and triangles. The evening was merry and hot but the heat seemed softer as the old village was canopied by the leaves of great shade trees along the bayou and throughout the village.

Outside the gates of the historic village, the first thing I passed on the way back to the hotel was an enormous petrochemical plant, the lights of its towers glowing mistily in the dense tropical heat. Around the towers splayed a huge, empty parking lot like a set of interlocking airport runways. After this, I came upon miles and miles of neon lights lining the six-lane road that I was driving on, so that in the flat Louisiana landscape it felt like I was driving down a man-made canyon. And I thought about the little show that I had just seen and it struck me that the dancers did not see themselves as engaged in anything heroic. They were just doing what they loved, but surrounded by the sprawl of asphalt and the cool capsule of my rented car, they seemed heroic to me.

In "Acadie du nord," poets like Hermenigilde Chiasson, Gerald Leblanc, and Dyane Leger have given words to the subconscious murmur of a people. But if the north is the pen of Acadie, the south is the dance. What Louisiana Acadians mean when they say a restaurant is good is that the band is good and there is room on the dance floor to move. The food is expected to be fine.

We use the same basic musical instruments—the violin, the guitar, and the accordion—in the north to make dance music, but it has a different rhythm. The music of the north is strongly influenced by the Scottish traditional jigs, reels, and strathspeys. Square dancing, step dancing, and a kind of hybrid swing that has no name are the dances that northern Acadians are adept at. "Les Acadians tropicales" favour the waltz, the two-step, and an endlessly inventive, very fast fox trot. I try to pick it up on the fly, but I can't quite get it. I'm not alone. When a northern group like Blou plays, all the Acadians "from the north" hit the dance floor and the

Louisiana Acadians stand and watch. When a southern band takes over, there is a changing of the guard as the southern Acadians get set to swing.

Who can dance the best?

Who can say?

Acadians love to dance, that's all. An Acadian fiddle player has to have a rock-solid dance beat. It's the same in Louisiana. There is no sitting around listening to the band quietly from the stands. The organizers of Louisiana's great closing concert, "Cri du Bayou," had to put a press release out to quash the rumour that no dancing would be permitted, that all people could do was listen. Once

> *Who can dance the best? Who can say? Acadians love to dance, that's all.*

the press release hit the radio waves, ticket sales begin to flow again.

I've always loved music and we've always had instruments and people to play them in the house, but it has taken Louisiana to make me realize that music is one of the great conduits through which cultures are both sustained and invented. At the street

dances, I watched young children dancing, playing in bands, singing in French, and it struck me with great force that knowing how to conjugate your verbs in impeccable Bescherelle style will never keep a culture alive, but music and song will. You have to want to sing in your language for it to continue.

At one of the village twinning ceremonies (where a village from

Louisiana is twinned with a village from Canada), I heard people in their fifties reading in public a language that they had always spoken but never read. I wish my own grandfather had had this chance. It would have made a difference, especially in his older years.

Nighttime in Louisiana was friendlier than daytime. At night, the sun's heat baked rather than burned. On the night of my last street party the Magnolia Sisters played, and their Louisiana-Cajun rhythms rose in the night to circle then disappear into the dark sky. The music and the heat mixed like a drug to anaesthetize all feelings as if, on this night, we were not *on* the turning earth but *were* the turning earth, and the turning earth was Louisiana. It was easy to feel its magic.

The bells of the church pealed out over the town square announcing the beginning of the tintamarre. The tintamarre is the parade held in the Acadian villages in Louisiana and in Maritime Canada each year on August 15, after the haying is over. People come out of their houses and bang pots, wear odd costumes and shout. No one knows why it is done. For years, it was just a memory, but in the last few years, there has been a revival. The tintamarre is now held again.

I had never been in a tintamarre parade before. I always thought of it through the English language, and in English one "has a parade." When a young woman announced from the street stage that "*Nous ferons la Tintamarre devant l'hotel de ville,*" it sent a thrill of recognition through me as I suddenly realized the difference between "having" a parade and "making" one. Just like *on fait la foin* (you make hay), tintamarre is something that is done together. I wanted to laugh out loud with delight at such a simple discovery.

The tintamarre in St. Martinville started at the town hall and wound back to the church for midnight mass. We stood in the street, banging on our pots, talking and singing, waiting for the mayor to give us the signal to begin. There were several hundred of us gathered there. On that night, at that time, all over Cajun

Louisiana, tintamarres were being made.

I had often wondered how it might feel to be in a tintamarre, if there was a right way to do it. I discovered that the right way was the last thing on my mind. I was content to bang on a pot with a wooden spoon and sing a song that I remembered from childhood. There was nothing harmonious about my song. I sang poorly, but that did not matter at all because the clash and bang of frying pans, cooking pans and pots of all kinds made every voice melodious. That made me smile even more.

I stood with a young Louisiana poet named Jambon, a French teacher in one of the immersion schools. I had heard him read earlier in the day. His poetry is exuberant, funny, and lyrical. We did not converse. He was content to bang on his pot and carry his Cajun-Louisiana flag, which he draped around his shoulders like a cape. I held a northern Acadian flag with a woman from New Brunswick who lives somewhere in the American mid-west. She sparkled with excitement and her excitement ricocheted off my own.

"Acadie tropicale," someone cried from the back of the parade and someone answered back, "Acadie du nord."

"Acadie tropicale."

"Acadie du nord."

Fragments of songs and phrases banged together in the mist of the hot night, like the sea banging against the shore. I thought: *I am a whale. I am a dolphin. I am a singer of great songs. I am a mote of dust in a thin ray of starlight. I am nothing but the sound of life, with no beginning and no end.* I felt a bubble of pure joy welling up inside of me. *This is better than chocolate, better than champagne. How is it*, I wondered, *that we are so happy?*

In the morning, I found a local diner for my last breakfast in Lafayette. It was alive with the hum of happy conversation, and the fragrant scent of frying bacon was in the air. I took a booth by a window. It felt like home. A waitress came striding up to my table. She was about my age, her hair streaked with gray, but her face light and lively. "What do you want, babe?" she asked. At fifty-three, this was not an unwelcome greeting. I replied that what I wanted was to come back to Louisiana.

CHAPTER NINE

The Wolf and the Lamb

Aide-toi, le ciel t'aidera.

Help yourself and heaven will help you.

—Jean de La Fontaine

My grandfather sent my father out into the world with this expression about helping yourself from Jean de La Fontaine, from a story called "Le Chartier Embourbé." La Fontaine (1621–1695) lived during the time of Evangeline's Acadia. Like millions of children before me, I learned to read through his re-telling of Aesop's fables. In my parents' home, these old stories were held in a big fat book decorated with large, colour illustrations of foxes and grapes, rabbits and tortoises, all of which seemed more real to me than people. The passage of years has not dulled my interest in the fables of La Fontaine—unlike almost all the other stories I read as a child, they have grown more intriguing and beautiful with age. Their sweet, complex wisdom still makes me smile. Even the unadorned statement at the close of "The Wolf and the Lamb" is one I still think about often.

In the story, a wolf comes upon a lamb drinking in a stream at the edge of the forest. The wolf accuses the lamb of dirtying the water. The lamb replies reasonably that he is downstream from where the wolf drinks so he can't be harming his water. The wolf complains that the lamb drank out of his river a year ago. The lamb replies that he couldn't have; he hadn't been born.

Then it was his brother, snarls the wolf. Impossible, the lamb replies, he doesn't have one.

The lamb always answers politely, deferring to this great "seigneur" of the forest and referring to him deferentially as "Majesty," but he stubbornly will not agree with the wolf's accusations. He continues to explain why the wolf is mistaken. Finally, in exasperation, the wolf says "I don't care. You and your kind have made my life miserable."

The wolf has been looking for, but cannot find, his *causus belli.* Finally losing patience, he does what he wanted to do all along: he kills and eats the lamb. (Modern political parallels are easy to find— the invasion of Iraq would be the most recent example.) The tale ends with the laconic observation that *la raison la plus fort est toujours la meilleure.* The most frequent translation of this line is "might makes right," but the one I have always liked the best is the literal one, "the reason of the strongest is always the best."

Perhaps Jean de La Fontaine made no moral aside here because he could see no alternative to the wolf eating the lamb. In the seventeenth century, this was the way of the world, and not only at court—an aristocrat could hang a peasant for killing a rabbit on his land. The link between the wolf and the lamb, the aristocrat and the peasant is not hard to see. The king could, with a simple *lettre de cachet,* throw someone he was annoyed with into a windowless dungeon cell until they died from cold and hunger. This is precisely what his representatives did in the New World. In Acadia, Nicholas Denys had good reason to run once the aristocrat D'Aulnay decided to go on the warpath. As the king's representative, D'Aulnay's power was absolute.

Jean de La Fontaine died in 1695. A hundred years on, the French aristocracy would be overthrown and the idea of running a country through laws created by democratically elected assemblies would be introduced and eventually cherished. This is the alternative that La Fontaine's fellow countrywoman, Marie Lineman, a French minister of housing, would refer to three centuries later when she stated at the World Social Forum in Porto Alegre that human beings are more than mere specks of dust in the universe, that as citizens people play a grander part in the human voyage than they ever could as individuals. Democracy is a unique and powerful social invention that permits the peaceful transfer of power from one group to another without war or bloodshed and that allows the lamb's view to be heard and sometimes even upheld. It was embraced by the Acadians fifty years or more before the French and American revolutions. By the time of the exile in 1755, the Acadians were already dealing with the feudal hierarchies of Britain and France via locally elected deputies who represented them to both the English in Halifax and to the French at Fort Beausejour. The Acadians never abandoned this commitment to a democratic society. They couldn't adjust to France when the deportation returned them to that country, where they referred to feudal society as the *ancien regime*. They took the ideals of democracy with them when they emigrated from France to Louisiana and found their way back to Canada, where they continued to elect their own deputies when they set up new communities. It explains why they embraced Canadian federalism from the outset and were quick to send members of parliament and senators to Ottawa to represent them.

As a boy, my father can remember Prime Minister Mackenzie King visiting Inverness, Cape Breton Island, during the height of the depression to make a campaign speech. This kind of effort to reach out, to be seen, to speak and listen to people was much appreciated. Unlike the Quebecois, the Acadians controlled no province of the Canadian federation and it was clear to them very early that the Canadian federal context was a new and useful political idea. And time has proved them right. Canadian federalism has been responsible for recognizing them as a people and has responded to local needs, building docks and roads, and enabling their children to be educated in the French language. Above all, federalism has enabled Acadians to feel included in the national fabric.

The problems that Acadians face today with the legitimacy of the federal system are no different than those faced by any other Canadian. At the root of these problems is the private sector's increasingly symbiotic relationship with democratic institutions, a relationship predicated upon two constants of both business and politics: power and money. But citizens are more than merely "consumers," more than "clients." Citizenship refers to the role individuals play in the governance of their society, and that role includes the voicing of honest and clear criticism of how well the government is fulfilling its role, not simply receiving a service.

CHAPTER TEN

The Seven Years' War, Evangeline, the Métis War and Globalization

The admiral was said to have left a fortune of 600,000 pounds, amassed in India, while Admiral Pocock is also very rich. Robert Clive was sending huge sums to London through Dutch merchants. Bengal was now secure for the production of wealth, be it for the East India Company or individuals.
—The Struggle for Empire, 1756-63, *Tom Pocock*

The exile of the Acadians is usually described in the context of Longfellow's romantic poem *Evangeline*. The poem is based on a story Longfellow heard about two young people being separated on their wedding day during the deportation. The figure of Evangeline, in her simple Breton skirt and bonnet, has emerged as a collective symbol for all things Acadian. There are Evangeline newspapers, insurance companies, drive-ins, parks, statues, churches, and songs, but the popularity of this sympathetic figure has obscured the reality of the Acadian deportation and its significance. And the reality is that the deportation of the Acadians wasn't unusual. It was common garden stuff. The only thing unique about it is that it was relatively non-violent. The deaths were entirely collateral—disease in refugee camps, ships sinking at sea and so on. There were no murders, no massacres.

Then why is the story of the Acadian exile so compelling? Because there was something utopian about life in Acadia before the deportation. They had the good fortune to live free of feudal chains at a time when most ordinary rural folk lived lives of semi-slavery. They were blessed with a clement climate and their dyke lands were extraordinarily rich. The bay on the other side of their dykes was stocked with mussels, clams, lobsters, haddock, halibut, and flounder. They fought with no one, had affectionate, respectful relations with their Mi'kmaw neighours, and had even managed to dodge the religious fundamentalism that had collared both Europe and North America. Most extraordinary of all, without an army, without fighting anyone, without a literate bourgeoisie, they had elected their own representatives and had come to think of themselves as their own people.

This is not romantic folklore. It is the common bric-a-brac of any history of Acadie, making the ultimate loss of the society and the landscape all the more sad. The Acadian deportation has happened over and over again in different guises to different people and for the same constellation of reasons. National and corporate commercial powers don't like and don't want strong, independent peasant cultures, be it the Mayan peoples of Middle America and Mexico, the Kurds of Kurdistan, the peoples of the Baltic States, the Basques, Chechens, Ukrainian Kulaks, the Ogani of the Niger Delta, the Amazonian River Valley native peoples, the Canadian Métis—the list could on for pages. Everywhere strong, distinct peasant cultures are suppressed with violence through deportations or displacements, massacres and civil suppressions by the nation state and global commercial interests. The stronger and more independent-minded the peasant culture is, especially if combined with valuable resources, the more violent the suppression.

Peasant cultures that want to control their own resources and create their own local administrative structures are not a happy idea for powerful governments, be they in Moscow, Beijing, Washington or London. The desire of the powerful is always to control the production of wealth or the sources of wealth.

The weapons of command and control have become more diffuse and complex since the eighteenth century. Smart bombs and night vision goggles have replaced the lumbering broadsides of British warships and the romance of telescopes on the poop deck, but the purpose and results of wars against peasant cultures remain the same.

The war of 1756–63, or the Seven Years' War as it came to be known, of which Evangeline and the Acadians were little more than collateral damage, was distinguished by its purpose and global reach. It was the first war that could be described as a "world war," being fought in the Philippines, India, North Africa, the Carribean and North America. Unlike earlier wars, it wasn't a religious war or a dispute between brawling aristocratic clans; it was a commercial war fought over access to human and natural resources, and although the protagonists were European with Britain, Prussia and Hanover on one side and France, Austria, Sweden, Saxony, Russia and Spain on the other, it was fought primarily in distant theatres. In defining a beginning point for commercial globalization and the planetary spread of capitalism, it would be hard to find a better start line than the Seven Years' War.

The Seven Years' War had little to do with who ruled in Europe or whether one was Muslim, Catholic, or Protestant. The British didn't care what religion the Indians practised as long as they could access the nation's wealth. Just as oil companies like Halliburton Industries today in Iraq are indistinguishable from the American civilian political administration (with officers of Halliburton like Dick Cheney moving seamlessly from chief executive officer at Halliburton to vice president in the White House), with the roles virtually indistinguishable, it was the same story during the Seven Years' War. And it was then the pattern would be set.

In 1756 the interests of the officers of the East India Company in Bengal and the Hudson's Bay Company in North America were inseparable from the interests of the British government. The French, Dutch and Spanish were no different, with mirror commercial companies like la Compagnie d'Inde. In the Seven Years' War, the resources fought over were slaves (Britain's greatest source of trade revenue), precious metals, spices, cod fish, sugar, citrus fruits, rum, and timber—sources of wealth for the profit of European companies.

The English prime minister, William Pitt, literally bankrupted the country fighting the Seven Years' War, but the financial consequences of winning were incalculable. They would catapult Britain from being just another brawling European nation into a world economic power controlling trade.

In India, the fit between commerce and the military was the tightest. There it was impossible to distinguish whether it was the East India Company or the British government that was physically fighting the war. Under senior officer Robert Clive, the company had its own small, private army and Clive fought most of the early land battles. He depended on the British navy to control his supply lines to Europe and keep the French supply lines in disarray—other than that he won all the initial battles, giving Britain control of Bengal and eventually all of India. The squabbles over the fabulous wealth that these victories generated for the admirals and East India Company officers would prove almost as lethal as the wars themselves, with Robert Clive eventually committing suicide over accusations and counter-accusations regarding the distribution of the spoils.

In North America, the fit wasn't quite so neat, but it was much the same story. The Hudson's Bay Company officers had fought naval battles with the French in Hudson's Bay for control of the fur trading routes since the eighteenth century. These battles continued after Britain won the Seven Years' War because although the peace treaty permitted the French Canadians continued access to fifty per cent of the fur trade, determining that share was impossible. The fur trade wars continued unabated well into the nineteenth century, until the British and French companies merged to mutual profit.

With twice the population of Britain, and more resources and allies, France should have won the war. But the aristocrats at Versailles could never quite get the external focus required to engage fully in a global conflict. Voltaire's famous reference to Canada as "quelques arpents de neige," (a few acres of snow) sums up a substantial part of French thinking about the world beyond the old continent.

Loyalty without bearing arms was a contradiction in terms for any British admiral, general or governor—even the Highland Scots had decided that fighting for George II was a good idea—so the idea of removing the Acadians before they could change their minds and become a serious military threat had long seemed a sane and sensible solution. When the moment arrived and the transport ships and the troops were finally at the governor's disposal, he did what the government of the day had long wanted to do—he dispersed the Acadians to the four corners of the globe to end forever the possibility of their community becoming an economic or political threat. Once they were gone, the governor sent in his agents to gather up the best stallions and cattle for his own and his friends' enterprises.

> *Once they were gone, the governor sent in his agents to gather up the best stallions and cattle for his own and his friends' enterprises.*

Except that this is not exactly the end of the story—it's simply one episode in a continuing story, in which the locale and circumstances change but the global tune remains the same. A century later, in the years 1868 to 1870, the Métis people of Western Canada were in exactly the same position. The Métis were an independent people who had well-established settlements directly in the way of the commercial interests of the Hudson's Bay Company in London and the nascent Canadian political administration in Ottawa. The Métis parishes

and villages at Red River and farther west along the South Saskatchewan River straddled the best land and were the funnel points through which all western settlement would have to flow. It was clear that the people who controlled the lands of these western gateways would quickly become rich as new immigrants arrived.

Like the Acadians before them, the Métis were farmers and hunters with enough sophistication to be able to form independent political positions, elect deputies, create local governments, and defend their rights to the lands they occupied. This was not a happy notion for John Macdonald's new government in Ottawa, which had gone to the expensive trouble of travelling to London to purchase these western lands from the International Finance Society (IFS). It was a purchase that didn't recognize any rights for the First Nations or Métis people who happened to being living there. They were sold along with the buffalo.

What strikes me most about the rebellions of 1868–70 and those in Saskatchewan in 1884 is not the details of the struggle, but how easily the pillaging of the Métis lands was justified to the Canadian public by characterizing the Métis desire to protect their lands through local self-government as a "rebellion." The Canadian motivation for the violent suppression and dispersal of these people was, on the other hand, presented as nothing more than the simple, peaceful desire for justice and to open the west for settlement.

The Métis suppressions are the *Evangeline* myth in a different guise, the destruction of a people to serve global commercial interests that had nothing to do with justice or opening up the west for settlement. In the land between deal the IFS—which had bought the Hudson's Bay Company in 1863—and the Canadian government, the IFS retained one twentieth of all the fertile land that would eventually be opened up for settlement and large land holdings around all of their forts, plus they received £300,000 pounds up front from the government. In this deal to end all deals, the IFS cleverly restructured its interests in Canada by off-loading onto the public sector the least profitable lands and parts of its operations (i.e. millions of marginal acres), and retained the most fertile and most profitable. The Canadian government received, cloaked in the transfer of £300,000 and "future interests" to the IFS, vast lands and the concomitant authority to do what it wanted with them. The west could have been opened up for settlement without the need for war against the Métis and their displacement. The Métis leaders never said they would resist the arrival of newcomers. But if the Métis communities and political organization had not been broken up by Macdonald, it would have been the Métis who would have controlled and benefited from that immigrant settlement. Instead, they were marginalized and impoverished by it. Simply put, the Métis would have made a lot of money and Sir John and his buddies would have made a lot less.

The "patriots" who fought Louis Riel, including the man who actually hanged him, became rich from the sale of real estate, while the men and women who supported Louis Riel were forced to flee south into the American territories or north into remote areas.

It took about twenty years to remove the Métis from the principal western trade and travel routes. It took eight years to dispossess the Acadians of their lands, beginning in 1755 and ending in 1764. The success of the deportation can be measured by the fact that after eighty years of resettlement, the Acadian Maritime population was still only at three or four thousand people; in 1755, it had been somewhere between thirteen and eighteen thousand.

In my struggle to discover Acadie and to figure out what it means to be Acadian, I have realized that the Acadian story is part of a much larger tale. My own family's history is shared with many others in many different places. I have come to the conclusion that there are few families without refugees in their family tree; it is a story with a relentless continuity.

Nothing essential has changed in the 250 years since the British and French fought vicious battles over military bases like Chandernagore and Pondicherry along the Indian Coast during the Seven Years' War. The war in Iraq has resulted in the destruction of numerous Kurdish villages, because they lay atop a precious resource—oil—and they made the mistake of wanting some economic and social control over and above commercial forces and military states. Less recently, the islands of Diego Garcia—part of the Chagos Islands in the Indian Ocean—became home to the US Navy and Air Force. But the Chagos Islands were once home to several thousand native inhabitants. These inhabitants were expelled between 1966 and 1973 when the US decided to lease the islands from the British, who acquired them during their colonial wars. As a condition of the fifty-year lease, the islands would be provided free of inhabitants—this for a discount on some American-made Polaris missiles. Expelled to islands thousands of miles away like Mauritius and the Seychelles, where they were not welcome and where no provisions for their re-settlement were made, the islanders received little or nothing in compensation for the loss of their islands and presently exist in destitute circumstances.

I was reminded of all this while watching George W. Bush twist and turn looking for a reason to invade Iraq. There was no overpowering reason for such an invasion, just as the UN weapons inspectors had told him. There was, however, an overpowering desire to "liberate" the oil resources of Iraq for Halliburton Industries. Just as there was an overwhelming desire to "liberate" western Canadian land within a development formula that could accrue profits to the IFS and the Government of Canada. If the Métis had been settled in a remote part of Hudson's Bay, they would have been of no interest to either the IFS or the Canadian government—until the government wanted their land for hydro development or minerals or whatever.

"*Plus ça change, plus c'est la même chose*" is an old French expression. The more it changes the more it's the same thing. But I don't think a philosophical shrug of the shoulders is good enough any more. We need to stop celebrating Evangeline and Louis Riel as national symbols of wronged virtue and start learning the whole stories of their respective histories.

But reclaiming the past isn't an easy thing to do. Three hundred and fifty years after the deportation, the Canadian federal government has finally admitted that the Acadian exile happened; the British government has yet to do the same. There are many practical, useful reasons for why the winning side is never interested in letting the "real" story get out, but this cycle can only continue if we let it.

Louis Riel was not fighting to maintain slave states. He was fighting for some simple, human rights—the rights of the Métis people to occupy their lands, to keep their communities intact, and to govern in local matters. (The same things the Acadians wanted.)

Although he put it much more eloquently than this, what he essentially said was: "You must understand there were two nations, one large and powerful, one smaller and less powerful, two unequal nations, but no less equal in rights."

His words remain as relevant today as they were in the days before he was hanged. Somehow, we must find a way to live together on this planet in a manner that sustains all peoples, not just the powerful.

CHAPTER ELEVEN

Leaving Home

There is a headland at Middle Cove
which juts into infinity
that waits for neither
the beginning, nor the end
of the universe
that has
welcomed countless mornings
and sealed evenings
beyond measure.

—from "The Debris of Planets," by Clive Doucet

There is a letter in my father's papers from Father DeCoste. It was written in 1945, just after World War Two had ended. The euphoria of that vast conflagration finally extinguishing could be felt even in the tiny village of Grand Étang. The letter is now more than fifty years old, dog-eared and faded. In it, the priest expresses his happiness that the war is over, and he looks forward to the day when the boys are home. What a difference that will make in the village!

It is easy to understand why my father has kept this letter all these years. The priest's simple affection for my father and the village is readily apparent. But my father did not come home to Grand Étang. He was part of a second exodus from Acadie, via the Veterans Assistance Bill, to attend university. 1945 is a long time from 1755, but there were connections to that first exodus of 1755 in both the character of the villages left behind and in the veterans' own characters. It had been two hundred years since the exile, but in spite of this long settlement, the villages of Acadie had remarkably little material wealth and few ties to the outside world.

Our old house in Grand Étang was beautiful, with views of the sea from every window, but the house itself had nothing more than was absolutely required: a bed and bureau in each bedroom, hardwood floors without carpets, hardback chairs for sitting. Very little had been bought from a store. The richness was in the people, in the stories and voices, in the music.

When Father DeCoste wrote to my father, his joy was not simply the joy of seeing the end to a terrible war, but the joy at the thought of a new beginning for Acadie, one where the poverty and isolation engendered by the exile would finally be defeated. But things didn't quite work out as the old priest expected. My father's generation came home only to visit, then they went away again—to Montreal, Toronto, Ottawa, London, out into the wide world.

During the 1940s, 50s and 60s, Acadie persevered, but without much of that in-between, school-educated generation. Men like my Uncle Philias, who stayed behind to teach high school, were unusual. Today, some people are still irritated that my father's generation abandoned Acadie for big-city careers. Nonetheless, the young men and women that went out into the world to compete found that they could do so very well. They became chief executive officers, scientists, medical doctors, university professors. Among them is a winner of the great Goncourt Literary Prize and a governor-general of Canada. And by reaching back to their villages with mature skills, ideas, and worldly contacts, the generation that left helped bring about an Acadian renaissance.

In the 1960s, an Acadian university at Moncton was built, the first full-spectrum university teaching not just liberal arts and theology, but pure and applied sciences, law, administration, health sciences, and business management. Acadian publishers, writers, musicians, and businesspeople selling books, songs and products around the world began to emerge.

Acadie has been inventing and re-inventing, losing and finding itself for four hundred years. The Acadie of the dyke farms and *Evangeline* was different from the Acadie of the fishing vil-

The Acadie of the dyke farms and Evangeline was different from the Acadie of the fishing villages of my grandfather and again from the Acadie of today.

lages of my grandfather and again from the Acadie of today. But then again, nations are always being invented, re-invented, lost and found: Roman legions drew Hadrian's wall across Britain; the 49th parallel as a border is as arbitrary as the next.

When Captain Germain Doucet, Sieur de la Verdure, first came to Port-Royal in 1632, France scarcely existed. He came as part of the entourage for two aristocrats, Isaac de Razilly and his cousin, Charles de Menou d'Aulnay. Both had close connections to the court of Louis XIII. In the eighteenth century, France was a royal domain, not a nation of republican citizens. There was no common language. Bretons still spoke Breton. South of the Loire Valley, people spoke Occitan, Catalan, Provençal, and Basque. It was not "Vive la France" but "Vive le Roi."

In the New World, the people who would come to think of

themselves as Acadians came from every duchy and corner of France: the Bastaraches from the Pyrenees, the De Forests from Flanders, the Bourgs from Normandy, the Gaudets from the Loire Valley, the Dugas from Languedoc (Toulouse). Both Huguenots and Catholics were among them and this led to some conflicts in the early days, but by 1713, these different origins and different religious beliefs had been resolved and the settlers thought of themselves as Acadians. A new identity had been forged.

In the centuries to come, I hope they will say of the Acadians that they were a small and fiercely independent people, a people who came to represent not a nation but an idea, the idea that it is possible to have a sense of a people, a place, a culture and language without an army; that it is possible to be victorious without wars, and that it is possible to realize the dream of a world without borders.

CHAPTER TWELVE

Lost and Found

There's no greater sorrow on earth than the loss of one's native land.
—Euripedes

O nce upon a time, in the village of my father and grand-father, there was a parish priest named Father DeCoste. He had been the parish priest for thirty-five years and was much loved. A well-educated man, he knew his Shakespeare as well as his Molière, and tutored village children in geometry, math, Latin, French and English. He was responsible for many young men successfully graduating from the one-room village school and moving on to university. Just as he was a teacher, he was a profoundly devout man and much concerned with his spirituality and that of his parishioners.

His church was on a cliff edge over looking the sea. It was a simple building and in the way of simple things, beautiful. It was a place where it was easy to believe in God. Balanced on a small plateau between green mountains and the grey-blue sea, the church felt like a small boat tethered at the planet's edge, ready to sail towards the infinite, celestial vault of the sky.

Like any good mathematician, Father DeCoste was familiar with Copernicus and the notion that the earth was just one more planet circulating in the sky around a small star called the sun. Yet, at the end of mass, standing in front of his church with the wind blowing at his vestments, the sea stretching out towards the horizon, it did not seem foolish to believe that there was a heaven beyond the sky.

The moment still remains vivid in my mind when I first began to realize that maybe heaven wasn't beyond the blue sky of the village. It was when Yuri Gagarin went flying off into space. Pictures of the cosmonaut began to appear in the newspapers. He was smiling. He was handsome. He was Russian. And then, the first pictures of Earth from space began to be published in the newspapers. The pictures showed no outlines of nations, no outlines of cities. There was no Paris, New York, not even any nations. There was just this great blue and white ball hanging in space like some vast, amazing Christmas ornament.

Father DeCoste died before Yuri Gargarin's flight into space. He was sixty-seven and had never even driven a car. He had always walked or driven about the village in a one-horse buggy. One day, his heart just stopped as he was walking from the presbytery to the church. In the village, it was said that Father DeCoste "died in the traces." This was what people said when a hard-working horse dropped dead between the shafts of a wagon.

The last horse that my grandfather raised from a foal died in the traces. From time to time, I still think about that foal. I saw him born and grow from a wobbly colt to a tall, strong three year old. He was an affectionate and noble fellow with a white blaze on his face, soft, brown eyes and a gentle spirit. He was the kind of horse that never shirked a day's work. I was very fond of him and sad when Grandfather decided to sell him to neighbours who needed a young horse. I saw him occasionally around the village, always putting his heart into the task. One winter day, his owners were driving him across the pond with a sleighload of logs. The ice split open under them, and the horse and wagon went into the icy water, where he drowned in the traces. Father DeCoste died like this, head down, straining against the traces, pulling his parishioners towards heaven.

Father DeCoste never got to see the photograph of the earth taken from space. What would he have thought of it? His only memorial is a pamphlet written and published by one of his students after he died. This little publication is called "Father Joseph Aloysius DeCoste, parish priest of St. Joseph du Moine, a personal appreciation."

I think about Father DeCoste quite often, because his passing is all mixed up in my mind with the passing of an age—the age of my grandmother and grandfather, the age of horse-drawn farms and fishermen going out on the sea in small boats, and my own father's youth.

In her single character play *La Sagouine*, Antonine Maillet uses a mop and a pail as the central metaphor for her heroine's life. (A mop and pail are the only props the actress has.) There is great integrity in the image, because it fairly represents a central reality in the lives of women like my grandmother, who had to care for populous households in the villages of Acadie—be they in Louisiana or Atlantic Canada—with very little help but their own muscle and wit. Even with an amiable husband, large families often meant much drudgery, and childbirth was more perilous than any man's work. To succeed in the Acadie of my grandparents' time, women and men alike needed great stamina, rock-solid good health, and good luck.

Grandfather's first wife died after the birth of their second child. I know her only from an old photograph, in which she looks to be barely out of her teens. Grandfather's second wife, Marie Hache, lost her first husband to tuberculosis. There were no antibiotics then and tuberculosis and the other great bacterial diseases killed not only cows but humans as well, in long and painful coughing deaths. People and cows just coughed until they died.

Thus, my grandfather and grandmother found themselves widower and widow before either were out of their twenties. Marie Hache was a first cousin to Grandfather's first wife and had no children of her own. Grandfather already had two little boys to take care of. I have no idea how much romance was in their connection, but there were certainly children, six more boys and two girls.

The men who succeeded at farming were the ones who could rise day after day at 5:00 a.m. and keep going until nightfall with

> *Hard work, death, disease, injury—no, the old life was not easy.*

only brief stops in between for meals. My grandfather was one of the lucky ones, for crippling injuries were common as grass. They could happen in the wink of an eye. Suddenly, a storm could blow up and men would be lost at sea, often within sight of the harbour. Even the most careful man could not protect himself from a fast-moving belt that suddenly released from a pulley, or a bait knife that sliced from fish head to arm.

Hard work, death, disease, injury—no, the old life was not easy. Then why do I look on it with such affection? Probably because I saw little of the hardship and a lot of the good. By the time I was tagging around after my grandfather, the seventeen people who used to inhabit the bedrooms of the old house had shrunk to three: Grandfather, Aunt Germaine, and me. And much of the daily grind of farm life had disappeared. The farm, like the family, had shrunk. There were just four milk cows, about ten young cattle in the hills, a few chickens around the house, a single energetic pig, a mare and her foal. There was still work to be done, but it was a leisurely round, rather than a relentless necessity.

We would load the wagon with some fence posts, fertilizer or feed, working hard, but there was always time to drift over to chat with someone passing by. Often, we ended up visiting, drinking hot

> *Often, we ended up visiting, drinking hot sweet tea, eating biscuits, talking.*

sweet tea, eating biscuits, talking. By then Grandfather's old house had been appointed comfortably with electricity, a refrigerator, hot and cold running water, and indoor plumbing. The wood stove remained in the kitchen, kept around for its soft, friendly heat.

The good that I saw was in the harmonious existence of a small farm and a small village. For all the hardships that life in a little farming and fishing village imposed on the people themselves, it was an environmental Shangri-la. No massive tractors ripped up the soil. Mono-culture did not exist. The word "organic" was not necessary to distinguish farming based on nature's biology from mining the land with seed and pesticide cocktails—all the farming was organic. Horses fuelled by hay and oats provided the power to till the soil. Cows were not penned in "milking parlours." Beef cattle did not stand all day in fetid feed lots, the bovine equivalent of chicken cages. Cattle roamed free until the snow flew and they decided on their own that they would prefer to be in the barn where it was warmer. Hens clucked and plucked around the house

and barn, seemingly happy and healthy in their daily round.

Times have changed, and there are no more villages like Grand Étang in Canada. The Third World, however, is full of Grand Étangs, and the globalized world is busy doing to them exactly what it did to Grand Étang—converting them or displacing them with mono-culture and factory farms. Every time another village is displaced by the global production line, the world's bio-diversity is lessened and we are made more vulnerable. The more a small people is forced to lay down its language and culture, the less diversity the world has and the poorer, less interesting we are.

During the great depression in the 1930s, Canadians from the urban centres and from the big western farms that had dried up and blown away in the dust storms went back to these little farms and little villages. In the 1930s, the villages of eastern Canada were filled to bursting. It was a time when people lived sparely, because these villages were poor and because the decade was poor. But at a time when many people died of starvation, in a village like Grand Étang everyone ate and everyone was warm.

The same drive to get rid of local economies that happened in Canada in the 1950s, 60s and 70s is now happening in Asia, in Africa, and in South America, where small independent food producers are being replaced by single cash crop activity. This fact is regarded by the IMF and the World Bank as "productive and progressive" because mono-culture cash crops create "capital," which allows nations to borrow from the IMF and the World Bank. They can then use the borrowed money to modernize their economies, and modernization usually means buying armaments and mega-projects (which in turn accelerates the destruction of traditional economies). The end result of mono-culture and capitalization is that the nation loses its sustainable economy, gains some out-of-date First World weapons, some asphalt, some electricity, and a debt it can never pay off.

In the end, finding Acadie has always been about more than discovering one small people's place among the peoples and cultures that circle the earth. When Acadians leave home, they take their music, their dance, their language, and their stories with them but they leave without national illusions, for Acadians have never been animated by the thought that they can lock themselves away separately behind some national frontier or under some missile umbrella, divorced from the destiny of others.

So, nothing has changed for me. Grand Étang is still my ideal place, but that ideal has grown. It has become bigger, more beautiful, more complex, until now it includes the whole earth. In small corners of that great place can be found the churches, poets, singers and fishermen of Acadie. While Acadians have always been stubbornly independent, hanging on to their language and ways of being against forces that wished them assimilated, they know viscerally that one's success cannot be separated from one's neighbour's success. This idea continues in my life today far away from Grand Étang. When I struggle in my city for a light rail system, a green and more sustainable alternative to more roads and parking lots, I am in a small way remaining faithful to the idea of Acadie.

Finding Acadie is about more than finding Acadie, it's about finding ways for places and nations to exploit less and sustain more. It's about creating places where people want to stay, not leave, for to be lost and found in Acadie is also to be lost and found on our planet, with all of its prosperities and poverties, comings and goings, peoples and languages, religions and nations. To be found is to be confident that we all have a bright future. To be lost is to despair for any future at all.

Appendix

Le Premier Papillon du soir
(version originale)

Pendant le crépuscule,
un petit flot de souris-chauves*
sort du grenier,
vole dans l'air,
ici et là
mendiant dans le ciel.
Elles ne semblent pas naturelles,
ni oiseaux, ni souris,
même le mot, les souris-chauves
est laid
et je cours vers Grand-maman
certain que les sauvages souris-chauves
peuvent me manger comme le fricot.

Grand-maman me cueille dans ses bras
calmes et sereins
comme un grand arbre qui abrite les graines.
Ne t'inquiète pas. Ne t'inquiète pas,
elle marmonne,
les souris-chauves sont belles,
sais-tu qu'elles apportent
la bonne chance?
elles sont les papillons du soir.

Je regarde avec prudence en haut
et je remarque bien qu'elles sont noires
et plus grandes que les papillons ensoleillés,
grand-mamman a raison,
elles volent comme les papillons.

---

*En Acadie on dit souris-chauve, pas chauve-souris.

Veux-tu savoir comment
elles sont devenues papillons du soir?
Parce que les souris-chauves
n'ont pas toujours su voler.

Oui, j'ai dit à voix basse,
encore effrayé par leurs silhouettes dans le ciel.

Il était une fois, une souris,
la plus petite souris dans le champ,
et tout le monde la taquinait.
Pire, beaucoup de monde voulait la manger.
Oui, la manger.

Les renards, les corbeaux, les hiboux
tous avaient envie de la souris.
C'était une vie de fuite et de peur.
Et un jour la plus petite souris,
des plus petites souris-chauves,
a décidé qu'il n'y avait qu'une solution,
il lui fallait apprendre à voler
comme les goélands, comme les aigles.
Dans l'air,
personne ne pourrait la déranger,
elle serait libre.

Donc, chaque soir
quand les corbeaux étaient endormis,
quand le renard était plus tranquille,
et avant que les hiboux soient sortis,
elle faisait son possible,
elle essayait de voler d'une petite roche
en battant ses bras commes des ailes,
comme les goélands, comme les aigles
et chaque soir, elle ratait son coup,
elle ne montait pas vers le ciel,
elle n'était qu' une folle petite souris-chauvve
dans un champ immense.

Pire, après un temps,
la vie de la petite souris
devenait de plus en plus précaire,
un corbeau a remarqué sa folie
et a commencé à la chasser.
Chaque soir quand elle sortait de son trou,
le corbeau attendait
et la pauvre, petite souris-chauve trouvait
encore son nez dans la terre,
pas dans le ciel.

Enfin un soir, poignée! le grand corbeau
a attrapé la petite souris dans son bec,
au dernier instant,
la souris a échappé au coup du bec mortel,
blessée et ensanglantée,
et terrifiée presque à mort.

Mais ses blessures se sont guéries
et elle voulait toujours voler.
Têtue, elle essayait encore
mais comme autrefois,
toujours sans le moindre succès.

Tout le monde dans le champ se moquait d'elle.
Les lapins, les autres souris,
les oiseaux, les insectes, le bétail
et tout le monde disait la même chose:
on a une folle souris-chauve dans notre champ,
bon dîner, Maître Corbeau.

Maître Corbeau souriant et prêt à manger,
attendait les sorties futiles du soir.

Et les animaux des champs avaient raison,
ça ne pouvait pas durer,
la vie de la souris devait finir
dans le ventre affamé de Maître Corbeau.

Un soir, le bon Dieu était de passage
et il a remarqué
cette petite guerre si inégale
entre le corbeau
et la petite souris-chauve.
Et tout à coup,
il a arrêté la bataille
en mettant Maître Corbeau dans un coin
et la petite souris-chauve dans un autre.

Mes enfants,
calmez-vous et dites-moi
ce qui se passe?

La petite souris-chauve a expliqué au bon Dieu
qu'elle voulait voler comme un goéland,
comme un aigle
et Maître Corbeau a expliqué qu'il voulait dîner.
Le bon Dieu a commencé à rire.
Il a ri si fort qu'il a créé un vent,
un vent qui a poussé la petite souris
à travers le paysage comme une feuille en automne
et la pauvre souris était si confuse,
qu'elle pensait - qu'elle volait.
Et elle a crié:
Regarde! Regarde! Je vole!

Le bon Dieu l'a entendu et Il a ri
même plus fort
jusqu'au point où les granges et les maisons
ont frissonné.
Enfin le vent s'est adouci et la petite souris
est arrivée à terre à moitié morte de terreur,
de peine et d'exultation.

Le bon Dieu a ramassé la petite souris
dans sa main
et a dit tout doucement,
tu es une brave petite souris,

la plus brave que j'ai jamais vue,
tu as le droit de voler
comme un aigle,
mais j'ai déjà un monde plein d'aigles.

Que faire?

Le monde a un surcroît d'oiseaux de tous types,
les canards et les oiseaux chanteurs
par millions;
mes champs sont plein de papillons.

Que faire?

Et Il pense à ce qu'Il peut faire.

Le crépuscule s'avançait vers la nuit
et soudainement
Il s'est rendu compte,
qu'Il n'y avait pas de papillon de soir.
Nulle part.
Puis, Il a soufflé très doucement
sur le petit corps de la souris-chauve,
très doucement,
et la petite souris s'est reveillée.
Elle s'est reveillée et a commencé à voler
avec ses grandes et nouvelles ailes
comme un papillon,
le premier papillon du soir.